Rhodes
Around Britain

West 175 Publishing

Rhodes
Around Britain

Gary Rhodes

Photographs by Anthony Blake

West 175 Publishing

West 175 Publishing

P.O. Box 84848
Seattle, WA 98124
Web site: www.greatfoodtv.com

Credits

West 175 Publishing Production Team

Publisher	Greg Sharp
Editor in Chief	Chris Rylko
Culinary Director	Jenny Steinle
Production Coordinator	Kate Terhaar
Cover Design	Kathy Kikkert
Design Modification	Kay Green
Proofreader	Mary Rose Sliwoski

This book is published to accompany the television series entitled Great Food which was first broadcast in 1998.

UK Version
Tested and edited by Wendy Hobson
Designed by Isobel Gillan and Tim Higgins
Illustrations by Kate Simunek
Photographs © Anthony Blake
Styling by Anthony Blake and Joy Skipper
Food prepared by Gary Rhodes
Cutlery and crockery provided by Divertimenti and Villeroy and Boch

This book was published to accompany the television series entitled
More Rhodes Around Britain which was first broadcast in 1995.

First published by BBC Worldwide 1995
Reprinted 1995 (five times),
© Gary Rhodes 1995

PRECEDING PAGES Gary preparing four of his favorite cod dishes (see pp.66–73)

Acknowledgements

My thanks to: David, Margaret and Joseph Levin; Celia and Martin Warbrick from Kitchens of Knightsbridge; Alice Portnoy from Neff UK; Anthony Blake and Joy Skipper; Nicky Copeland and Wendy Hobson; Clare Adkins; the More Rhodes Around Britain production team; my *sous*-chefs, Stuart Busby and Wayne Tapsfield, and everyone at The Greenhouse; and of course, my wife, Jenny.

Library of Congress Cataloging-in-Publication Data
Rhodes Around Britain/Gary Rhodes; photographs by Anthony Blake - 1st U.S. ed.
p. cm.
Includes index.
Published to accompany the television series entitles Great Food.
ISBN 1-884656-07-2
1. Cookery, British. 2. Cookery, Great Britain. I. Great food (television program) II. Title.
TX717.R45 1998   98-34995
641.5941—dc21   CIP

Printed in Singapore
1 2 3 4 5 6 7 8 9 10
First U.S. Version

DISTRIBUTED BY PUBLISHERS GROUP WEST

Contents

But Everyone Knows
the British Can't Cook . . .

Of course it's enjoyable to have something to laugh about concerning the Brits.

All those centuries when Englishmen were running about the world conquering countries and making everyone wear linen dresses and serve tea at 4:00 p.m. gave them such a smug attitude. It feels great to be able to say, "Well, that's all very well but their entire dinner menu consists of mashed potatoes and minced meat pies."

Well, after reading these recipes from Gary Rhodes, we better find another culinary topic for jokes.

Now Gary Rhodes is seriously British. In the television series, Great Food, *you can watch Gary travel up and down the British Isles searching for the authentic flavors that were the basis for traditional British food.*

But any resemblance to bland mashed potato pies ends there. Gary's spiked hair style should be your first warning that he's up to something very modern. He says he isn't interested in just giving people traditional British food, as much as he wants to re-invent it.

So, drop your prejudices at the door and get ready to see the food of Great Britian with new eyes. For Merrie Old England is currently the land of culinary renaissance: a whirl of great chefs who take pride in cooking food that makes the whole world flock to their restuarants and pubs.

Gary Rhodes is at the forefront of this renaissance. I guarantee after one read: you'll never think of British food the same way again.

Bon appetit, or in the words of the British, "Eat up, Bloke."

Editor in Chief, CHRIS RYLKO

Introduction

"Food glorious food.
Hot sausage and mustard.
While we're in the mood
Cold jelly and custard.
Pease pudding and saveloys
'What next?' is the question ... "

Wonderful lines from "Food Glorious Food" from Lionel Bart's musical *Oliver!*, based on Charles Dickens' brilliant novel. It's a stunning musical, and what a wonderful question: What next?! Well, these lines sum up everything I feel about the most basic dishes. For me, all food can be glorious and that certainly includes sausages and mustard, or cold jelly and custard (you'll find my recipes for these in this book!).

This is the story this book wants to tell you – good food doesn't have to be played with or overdressed; all it needs is to be put together simply and well. And, like the musical, I hope you're going to be asking for more! And *Rhodes Around Britain* will give you more dishes to enjoy, more styles to try and a lot more options and scope with your cooking.

Over the years I have been in this industry, I have seen and learnt many things, but one thing that never seems to change is that too many chefs stick to strict rules and regulations. They create dishes and record recipes with with no room for change or variation. Well that's not what I want, or what this book wants to give you. I want to give you a lot more "roads" to choose from, and whichever one you follow is going to be up to you.

Cooks' attitudes and feelings about cooking styles change with experience. Almost all chefs started their careers at a catering college or culinary school. It's at these schools that we, hopefully, learn all or most of the basics about cooking. Then it's time to hit the industry – and the learning program starts all over again. But it so often happens that as chefs get to know dishes, they write them down and hide them. Of course, years on a lot of these recipes are shared in all kinds of cookbooks, but in so many of them, the rules are strict. This is the recipe and that's it!

The way I have written this book is designed to help break that pattern. I want you to read it very differently from other cookbooks. The recipes here are all reliable favorites of mine, and I hope will become favorites of yours, too. But every recipe involves room for movement and improvement! You can follow them, you can change them, use them as guidelines, follow the alternatives – the point is, it is up to you. There's a wealth of options beyond the recipes themselves.

Let's try a "for instance." If you happen to be reading a recipe and think, "that sounds tasty" but haven't got the time to start making, say, a fresh custard or fruit coulis, don't be put off. Just look at the alternative simple method – use ready-made custard mix with canned fruits or ready-made preserves, add a dot of fresh cream and, "hey presto," you have a delicious ice cream mix. Then, if you are saying to yourself, "But I don't have an ice cream machine," that's still no problem – the recipe will give you an alternative churning method. So everything is flexible – ingredients and methods. And the results? Well, I wouldn't offer you anything but the best!

Of course, I'd love it if you are able to try out some of the traditional methods – it may even surprise you how straightforward they are – but I live in the real world. Not everyone has the time to spend in the kitchen, but they do want excellent food, and there is no reason to compromise there. So, knowing you can eat great food whichever road you choose, have the confidence to adapt and you'll feel excited about trying out these recipes.

My cooking styles have certainly changed over the past fifteen years, which is all part of the learning process. You eventually find the style that suits you, adapting and absorbing from experience and turning it all to your own style. Even though my methods of cooking are still changing, I feel they will always be predominately British-based.

Traveling around Britain has been a lot of fun and almost a culinary education trip. It's been great to meet so many different people who get really excited and are so enthusiastic about good, simple, British dishes. One of the beauties of talking to so many people about cooking is you find out what the public are looking for and what everybody expects and wants from the industry. Giving people tastes and textures that they have never experienced and a style that's new is a great feeling, but what excites me even more is cooking dishes which evoke half-remembered taste sensations.

I don't cook for the food guides any more. I cook for the people, giving them food they are going to enjoy and not being afraid of serving anything, providing I'm convinced it can be cooked and eaten at its very best. I would love to promote British cooking around the world and to answer all our critics, because I have confidence in the dishes and the cooking styles we have to offer. It's all about believing in the recipe, knowing when a new dish is right, not adding anything that needn't be there, understanding ingredients and tastes that will complement each other.

I've included several "feature" dishes in this book. When first putting this book together, I wasn't quite sure of this structure, it almost seemed like an excuse for giving similar recipes. But after some thinking I said to myself, "If you've got ideas, then share them." The whole idea of the features is to give you a variety of recipes, some developed along a theme or style, so basically you'll find loads of cakes, ice creams, risottos, savory tarts and more – are you hungry? I hope so.

Filming television shows for *Great Food* has given me lots of new experiences in the culinary world – from cooking and training with Manchester United, being serenaded over cod, chips and mushy peas by the Nolan Sisters, driving a bright yellow Lotus, and cooking on an oil rig, to mixing with ostriches, singing to pigs, meeting on lighthouses and even being Gary Glitter's "Leader of the Gang" – and what's next?

Well, first have a go at some of these recipes. They'll excite you and you'll be the one saying to all your guests, "Just look at that!"

GARY RHODES

Notes on the Recipes

The basics of cooking don't change. Obviously we all try to develop new recipes and some new methods, but for most stocks, sauces or pastries it's "back to basics." So you'll find that I've included a few classic recipes in this book that appeared in my first cookbook, Chicken Stock and Veal *Jus* for instance. There are also recommendations for some ready-made products which remain the same. These are the foundations. I can promise you that everything else we do will be excitingly different!

You may find these few pointers useful when you start cooking.

1. Eggs are medium.
2. Wash fresh produce before preparation.
3. Spoon measurements are level.
4. If you substitute dried for fresh herbs, use only half the amount specified.
5. Unless otherwise stated, "season" or "seasoning" simply means seasoning with salt and pepper.
6. For information on alternative recipes for Veal *Jus* and stocks, see page 226.
7. If shallots are not available, substitute with half the quantity of onions.
8. I recommend Giradelli chocolate where recipes call for "good quality semi-sweet chocolate."
9. When I mention "to grease and season a baking sheet," it simply means to sprinkle the greased sheet with salt and pepper.

Soups & Starters

In my London restaurant, appetizers are critical to making a good first impression with my guests. Well, I think these recipes are brilliant! In fact, if you watch me on my television show, *Great Food*, you know I recommend making these appetizers in larger quantities to be main courses. They're really that good!

ABOVE *Griddled Scallops with Crispy Eggplant (see p. 42).*
LEFT *Grilled Tuna with Salsa Dressing (see p. 34).*

All the recipes have been developed to give everybody plenty of scope and movement – some have also "mini-features" so they include more than one dish in the basic recipe. There's everything from vegetarian to risottos and meat dishes – so I hope there's something to suit everybody and every occasion. So whether it's a light lunch you need, a summer barbecue, or special dinner party – there's something here for you.

And don't forget that I don't want you to stop with these recipes. All the recipes should be an inspiration and spark off stacks of ideas of your own. So if you want to make the leek and Parmesan risotto but add asparagus and strips of smoked salmon and even top with a poached egg, why not?

The majority of starters are fish-based, ranging from mackerel and salmon to scallops, cockles and smoked eel. Fish is one of the bonuses of England's island-living; we have such wonderful fish available to us. In fact, only the tuna and king prawns are not locally fished. I didn't go out of my way to give mainly fish starters, but I do think fish starters with meat main courses does suit many peoples' way of eating.

Gazpacho

This is a wonderful summer soup that has so many variations. My version has plenty of flavors and textures (see pp. 18–19). Gazpacho can be served chunky or puréed in a food processor or blender and served smooth. It is traditionally served with everything raw, but if you want to make a winter Gazpacho, then just cook the ingredients in the olive oil first, then add the tomatoes and the rest of the ingredients to give you a spicy tomato and sweet pepper soup. To make the soups totally vegetarian, simply replace the Tomato Coulis and Chicken Stock with tomato juice.

SERVES 4

1 lb (450 g) ripe plum tomatoes	2 tablespoons red wine vinegar
1 red bell pepper	1/3 cup olive oil
2 green bell peppers	1¼ cups Tomato Coulis (see p.232)
1 yellow bell pepper	1¼ cups Chicken Stock (see p.222)
1 cucumber, peeled and de-seeded	Salt and freshly ground black pepper
1 garlic clove	6-8 fresh basil leaves
1 onion	12-16 fresh tarragon leaves
2 teaspoons tomato paste	

Remove the core from the tomatoes, then plunge them into boiling water for 8-10 seconds. Transfer to cold water and slide off the skins. This is called blanching. Once the tomatoes have been blanched, halve and de-seed them. Remove the stalks and seeds from the peppers. The tomatoes, peppers, cucumber, garlic and onion can now be finely diced or puréed in a food processor or blender.

Mix together the tomato paste and red wine vinegar. Whisk the olive oil slowly into the paste. Now add three-quarters of the tomato coulis and chicken stock. Stir in the diced or puréed ingredients and check the seasoning with salt and pepper. Coarsely chop the basil and tarragon leaves and add them to the soup.

The soup can be as thick or thin as you wish. If you want to make it thinner, then add the remaining tomato coulis and stock.

Variations

A slice of white bread can be puréed with the vegetables to give a thicker texture.

The flavor of the soup can be made hotter and more spicy by adding a few drops of Tabasco or Worcestershire sauce or even both.

Green Lentil Soup

This soup is a good winter dish. I personally like to eat it any time of the year, but on a cold winter evening a large bowl of this soup served with plenty of crusty bread in front of the fire (are you getting hungry?) is absolutely delicious. I also like to add some smoked bacon to this soup to lift the flavor and almost make it a main course dish. It can, of course, be a vegetarian soup by simply omitting the bacon and replacing the chicken stock with vegetable stock.

SERVES 4

2 tablespoons unsalted butter	1 cup green dried lentils
1 tablespoon olive or vegetable oil	3¾–5 cups Chicken Stock (see p.222) or
2 large carrots, diced	Vegetable Stock (see p.223)
2 onions, diced	Salt and freshly ground black pepper
2 celery stalks, diced	⅔ cup milk or heavy whipping cream
4 slices smoked bacon, cut into strips	(optional)

Melt the butter with the oil. When the butter begins to bubble, add the diced vegetables and bacon and cook for 2–3 minutes without coloring. Add the lentils and continue to cook for a few minutes. Add 3¾ cups of the stock and bring to a simmer. The soup can now cook slowly, just simmering for 45–60 minutes.

The lentils must be cooked all the way through, becoming tender and thickening the soup. If the soup is a little too thick, add the remaining stock. This is now a lentil broth. To help the lentils become more evenly spread through the soup, purée gently with a hand blender or in a food processor or blender to give a thick broth consistency with the bacon and vegetables not totally broken. Alternatively, the soup can be totally blended to a purée, in which case you'll need to add a lot more stock. Season to taste.

To finish either of the soups, you can add the milk or heavy cream to give a slightly creamy texture.

Cream of Onion Soup

This is a very simple soup to make using just a few basic ingredients. It's delicious served with thick slices of toasted French baguette, finished with melting Cheddar or Parmesan. I like to serve it with Parmesan croûtons. Make these by slicing the crusts off a loaf of bread – any type you like: white, wholewheat, olive or anything else – and cutting it into ½ inch (1 cm) dice. Cook the bread in a roasting pan with just enough olive oil to cover the pan in a pre-heated oven at 400°F (200°C). As the croûtons are heating they will become golden and crispy. Every 1-2 minutes, turn the bread croûtons over to give an all-round color. Once the croûtons are totally golden and hot they can be sprinkled with finely grated Parmesan and mixed to give an overall cheesy taste.

Serves 4

4 tablespoons unsalted butter
1½ lb (675 g) onions, diced
2-3 celery stalks, diced
1 small potato, diced (optional)
1 leek (white only), diced

1 small garlic clove, chopped
3¾ cups Chicken Stock (see p.222) or
    Vegetable Stock (see p.223)
2 tablespoons heavy whipping cream or
    milk (optional)

Melt the butter in a pan. When the butter begins to bubble, add all the vegetables and cook for 8-10 minutes over a medium heat without coloring. Add the stock and bring to a simmer. Continue to cook for 20-30 minutes. The soup can now be puréed in a food processor or blender, then pushed through a sieve. If the soup is very thick, thin it down with a little extra stock.

As an extra, stir in the heavy whipping cream or milk to help the consistency and make a good cream of onion soup.

Lobster Bisque

Lobster bisque is regarded as the king of all soups and I don't think I can or want to argue with that. It is so rich in flavor and texture that it is really worth every effort in making it. If you make this quantity, you can freeze what you don't need.

Like all recipes, other flavors can be used. Crab, prawns or shrimp will all give you a full flavor. I use the same recipe to make a crab bisque to go with Crab Risotto (see p.60).

This recipe also holds lots of little extras – saffron, brandy, fennel – which all help to make this a better soup but can be left out for a basic bisque.

MAKES about 10 cups

1(1 lb) (450 g) lobster	A few fresh tarragon leaves
8-10 cups Fish Stock (see p.221)	A pinch of saffron
4-6 tablespoons unsalted butter	6 ripe tomatoes, quartered
1 tablespoon olive oil	¼ cup brandy
2 large carrots, diced	1½ cups white wine
4 shallots or 2 large onions, diced	⅓ cup long-grain rice
2 celery stalks, diced	Salt and freshly ground black pepper
1 leek, diced	A pinch of cayenne pepper
1 fennel bulb, diced	⅔ cup whipping cream (optional)
1 garlic clove, crushed	A few drops of lemon juice or brandy
A few fresh basil leaves	(optional)

If you are using a live lobster, bring the fish stock to the boil and drop in the lobster. Cook for about 5-6 minutes, then remove from the heat. The best way now is to leave the lobster in the stock until completely cooled. This will help flavor the stock and keep the lobster meat moist. If you are going to remove the lobster from the stock immediately, cook for 6-8 minutes, remove the lobster from the pan, then allow it to cool slightly before breaking the shell. Make sure you keep the cooking liquid to use in the soup.

Break off the claws and crack them with the back of a heavy knife to remove the lobster meat. Split the body and tail through the middle lengthwise and remove the tail meat. Reserve the meat to garnish the soup. The lobster shells are used to flavor the soup itself. I prefer to crack the lobsters down (with a rolling pin) in a large saucepan as finely as possible, making sure I get the maximum taste. It's also possible just to break the shells down without finely crushing them.

Melt the butter with the olive oil. Add the roughly chopped carrots, shallots or onions, celery, leek and fennel with the crushed garlic, basil and tarragon leaves. Add the pinch of saffron and the tomatoes and cook for a few minutes. Add the crushed lobster shells and cook for a further few minutes. Add the brandy and boil to reduce until almost dry. Add the white wine and continue to reduce. Add 8 cups of stock, bring to the simmer and continue to simmer for 20 minutes.

Add the rice and bring back to the simmer for 20-25 minutes. The rice should cook until overcooked to create a starch and thicken the soup. Check the soup for seasoning with salt, pepper and a pinch of cayenne pepper. The bisque can now be puréed in a food processor, with the lobster shells, to cream the soup, then pushed through a fine sieve. You now have a good, rich lobster bisque. The soup should be reasonably thick, well coating the back of a spoon. If it's very thick, add some more stock until you have the right consistency.

Always when making soups taste for seasoning once finished. Adding the cream, and a few drops of lemon juice or extra brandy, will always lift the taste.

Variations

This recipe works well with crab, prawns or shrimps. If you want to make a shrimp bisque, use either 1 lb (450 g) of good quality shrimp or 1 lb (450 g) of shrimp shells. The same applies to prawns.

If it's crab bisque you are making, just use the same preparation and cooking methods. Once the claws have been cracked and the meat removed, the flesh from the remaining two joints can be taken out with the back of a spoon. All the white meat should be kept to garnish the soup, and all the shell and brown meat can be broken and used for the soup. If you want to keep the brown meat, simply remove the central undershell and scrape out all of the inside.

OVERLEAF *Mussel Chowder in the foreground (see p. 20),*
Gazpacho (see p. 13) and
Gary making Cream of Onion Soup (see p. 15).

Mussel Chowder

Chowder is an old dish that was (and still is) a complete meal made with mussels, onions, potatoes and pork all cooked together (see pp. 18–19). It was originally made with cider or white wine but over the years milk and/or cream were added instead. This recipe has two stages: the first one tells you how to cook the mussels and the second is for the finished soup. Mussels, of course, can be bought already cooked. The vegetables and white wine are an optional extra which will give more flavor to the stock; you can just cook the mussels in the hot fish stock. If you are just using water, increase the quantity of mussels to1½ lb (675 g).

For the Mussels

1 carrot, roughly chopped
1 onion, roughly chopped
1 celery stalk, roughly chopped
½ leek, roughly chopped
1 bay leaf

2 tablespoons unsalted butter
¾ cup white wine
3 cups Fish Stock (see p.221) or water
1 lb (450 g) fresh mussels, washed and
    bearded

For the Chowder

4 tablespoons butter
4-6 slices bacon, cut into
    1 inch (2.5 cm) pieces
2 large potatoes, cut into ¾ inch (2 cm)
    dice
3-4 large onions, cut into ¾ inch (2 cm)
    dice

2 celery stalks, cut into ¾ inch (2 cm) dice
2½ cups mussel stock, Fish Stock (see
    p.221) or water
1¼ cups hot milk
⅔ cup whipping cream
Salt and freshly ground black pepper

To cook the mussels, cook the vegetables with the bay leaf in a little butter without browning until just beginning to soften. Add the white wine and boil to reduce until almost dry. Add the stock and bring to the boil. Add the mussels and cook for a few minutes until the shells open. Discard any that do not open. Drain off the mussels, reserving the strained cooking liquid.

Melt the butter in a hot pan and add the bacon pieces immediately. The pan must be kept hot to fry the bacon, allowing it to become golden; this will bring out the flavor of the bacon. There may be some bacon residue sticking to the base of the pan. Don't worry about this; it will give a good flavor to the soup. Once the bacon is colored, add the diced potatoes, onions and celery and cook, without coloring, for a few minutes, reducing the heat of the pan. Add the mussel or fish stock or water and bring to the simmer. Continue to simmer for about 20 minutes or until the potato is cooked but not breaking too much. The stock will have reduced a little, increasing the flavor. Add the hot milk and whipping cream and bring back to the simmer, checking the seasoning with salt and pepper. Add the mussels and warm for 1-2 minutes before serving.

Onion and Anchovy Pastry Pieces

These are lovely little appetizers: the strength of the anchovy contrasting with the rich sweetness of the onion on crisp puff pastry. To achieve the rich sweetness of the onions they must first be caramelized, a slow process but worth it.

SERVES 4

4–8 large onions, sliced	1 egg, beaten
1 tablespoon water	4 oz (100 g) canned anchovy fillets,
Salt and freshly ground white pepper	drained
6 oz (175 g) Puff Pastry (see p.212)	Olive oil

Place the onions and water in a large pan and place over a very low heat and keep on a low heat for anything between 2 and 4 hours. This process allows all the natural juices and sugars from the onions to be released. Once the onions have really softened and broken down, the sugar content will slowly start to caramelize. The onions will start to change color and are only ready at a deep golden stage. Season with salt and pepper.

Meanwhile, roll out the puff pastry very thinly and cut into 1 inch (2.5 cm) wide strips. Rest it in the refrigerator for 30 minutes to prevent it from shrinking.

Pre-heat the oven to 425°F (220°C) and grease a baking sheet.

Place the strips on the baking sheet and brush with beaten egg. Spoon some onions down the center of the strips, leaving ⅛ inch (3 mm) down each side. Lay the anchovy fillets head to tail down the center of the onions. Bake in the pre-heated oven for 8-10 minutes until the pastry is golden and crispy. Sprinkle with olive oil and cut into 1 inch (2.5 cm) squares. Serve at once.

Potato and Parsnip Chips

We all like chips with lots of different flavors (although some of them I'm not so sure about!), but you can't beat homemade salted chips with no other tastes to spoil. If you're having a dinner party and want something to go with pre-dinner drinks, then have a go at these. The parsnip chips are brilliant, just deep-fried slices of parsnip, as easy as that! They eat well dipped in Cranberry Sauce (see p.239).

SERVES 4

2 large potatoes, peeled	Oil for deep-frying
2-3 large parsnips, peeled	Salt

Pre-heat a deep fat frying pan to 350°F (180°C).

Shape the potatoes into neat cylinders, then slice them very, very thinly. Dry the slices on a cloth and fry a handful at a time until crisp and golden all the way through. Lift out and shake off any excess oil, sprinkle with salt and serve. The chips will stay fresh and crisp for a few hours, or longer if kept in a sealed container. Always make sure you eat them within 24 hours.

For the parsnips, just slice very thinly lengthwise and cook as for the potato chips until golden all the way through. Lightly salt and serve. The parsnip chips eat well dipped in cranberry sauce!

Duck Rillettes

Duck Rillette is almost like a homemade coarse pâté. You can make it with pork or goose, as well.

Other flavors can be added to the duck before cooking to help flavor the cooking fat which will be used to hold the duck together. Orange peel can be left in (as for canard à l'orange), or a clove of garlic, a bay leaf and sprig of fresh thyme. It's also possible to add some chicken or duck stock to this recipe for a moister flavor.

Duck Rillettes are best served with slices of thick, hot toast.

SERVES 4

4 duck legs   2 lb (900 g) duck fat
2 teaspoons rock sea salt

To make the rillette, simply follow the recipe for Confit of Duck (see p.88), cooking for a minimum of 2 hours. The duck meat has to be very tender and on the point of being overcooked.

Once cooked and still warm, take the duck legs from the cooking fat and remove the skin. Take all the meat from the bone, then break down the duck flesh, pulling it apart with two forks so that the meat is shredded rather than making a purée. Once the duck is reasonably finely shredded, start to add some of the strained cooking fat. This will give the meat a coarse pâté texture. After ⅔ cup has been added, check the seasoning with salt and pepper; season generously as they will be served cold. The duck rillettes should be moist and rich to eat. More fat can be added to make the pâté even richer (1¼ cups would be the maximum for this recipe). Spoon the rillettes into individual ramekins or one larger bowl and set in the refrigerator.

Once set, spoon a little of the liquid fat on top of the rillettes and allow to set. This will keep the rillettes fresh as long as they are chilled. I suggest, however, that you keep them no longer than a week. Because of the high fat content the pâté will set quite firm in the refrigerator so take out about an hour before eating to appreciate the full flavor.

Potted Salmon

This is a good summer dish which can be made and set in a serving dish and used as a starter or main course. Always be careful when cooking salmon as the fish is delicate. It needs very little cooking and should always be pink in the center to keep it moist and succulent.

To make the clarified butter, simply melt 1½ cups of unsalted butter until it foams, then the foam dies. Don't allow it to brown. Remove from the heat and leave to stand until the milky residue sinks to the bottom. Strain off through muslin.

You can make the salmon pots a few days in advance, but always serve them at room temperature. This will allow the butter to become softer and a lot tastier.

SERVES 4

1 lb (450 g) salmon fillet	Freshly ground white pepper
1¼ cups clarified butter (see above)	1 tablespoon chopped fresh parsley
2 shallots, finely chopped	1 tablespoon chopped fresh tarragon
1 small garlic clove, crushed	A few salad leaves
½ teaspoon ground mace	1 lemon, cut into wedges
½ teaspoon salt	Warm toast to serve

Trim the salmon fillet and cut into ½ inch (1 cm) cubes. Warm the clarified butter to simmering point and add the chopped shallots. Cook for a few minutes until the shallots have softened. Add the garlic, mace, salt and pepper. Carefully spoon the salmon into the butter and return to a *low* heat. The salmon can now only be stirred very carefully to avoid breaking. As soon as the salmon has a light opaque color, after about 5-6 minutes, remove it from the heat and allow to cool. Add the chopped parsley and tarragon.

Spoon the salmon into individual 3 inch (7.5 cm) ramekins, making sure that the shallots and herbs are evenly distributed. Top up with the remaining butter. You may find that you have some butter left. This can be used for cooking fish, or frozen until the next time. Cool and chill until set.

Remove from the refrigerator and allow to return to room temperature. Turn out the salmon onto plates and garnish with salad leaves and lemon. This dish also eats well with warm thick toast.

Mackerel Croquettes

These croquettes can be made with other fish: salmon, cod, prawns or shrimps. In this mackerel recipe, I've added one small fillet of smoked mackerel. This is not essential, but it does enhance the whole flavor of the fish without being overpowering.

Serves 4-6

4 mackerel fillets, skinned
2 shallots or 1 small onion, finely
    chopped
Salt and freshly ground white pepper
¾ cup white wine
1 bunch of green onions, chopped
1 smoked mackerel fillet
1-1½ cups or ¼ recipe Mashed Potatoes
    (see p.133), without milk, butter or
    cream

Cayenne pepper
2 tablespoons all-purpose flour
1 egg, beaten
1 cup dried breadcrumbs
2 tablespoons unsalted butter and
    cooking oil or oil for deep-frying
1 lemon or lime, cut into wedges
1 recipe Lemon Butter Sauce (see p.228)

Pre-heat the oven to 400°F (200°C) and butter a roasting pan.

To remove the central bones from the mackerel fillets, cut either side of the bones straight through the fish. This will leave eight strips of mackerel. Sit the fish on the pan with the chopped shallots, and season with salt and pepper. Add the white wine and cook in the pre-heated oven for about 6-8 minutes; the mackerel should only be just cooked. Drain off any excess liquid into a small pan, bring to the boil and boil to reduce by at least half. When the liquid has reduced, add the chopped green onions and cook for 30-60 seconds until only just beginning to soften.

Flake the smoked and cooked mackerel fillets and add the green onion reduction. Fold in 1 cup of the mashed potatoes which will be enough to bind. The texture can be loosened by adding more potato. Season with salt and cayenne pepper. Shape into balls or croquettes about 2½ × ¾ inches (6 × 2 cm). Leave to chill in the refrigerator.

Dust the croquettes lightly in flour, then pass through beaten egg. Roll in breadcrumbs and re-shape gently, if necessary, with a palette knife. To shallow-fry, heat the butter and oil over a medium heat and fry for 2-3 minutes until golden on all sides. To deep-fry, heat the fat to 300°F (150°C) and fry until golden. Serve with lemon or lime wedges and lemon butter sauce.

Variations

Sour cream flavored with fresh lime juice, salt and pepper makes a tasty dip.

Fillet of Mackerel with Caramelized Onions and Sweet Peppers

In this recipe, the mackerel is "cooked" in a sousing liquid made with white wine, white wine vinegar and water and flavored with pickling spices, star anise and herbs. The combination of the sharp, soused taste and the sweetness of the onions and peppers works really well. I like to present this dish on very thin short pastry discs. This gives the dish another texture, almost like eating an open tart.

Serves 4

1 recipe Shortcrust Pastry (see p.211)
4 mackerel fillets, skinned and trimmed
2 tablespoons Basic Vinaigrette (see p.241)

A few drops of balsamic vinegar
2 teaspoons fresh chives, snipped
  ½ inch (1 cm) long

For the Peppers and Onions

4 large onions, sliced
1 tablespoon water
1 large red bell pepper, cut into strips

1 tablespoon olive oil
Salt and freshly ground black pepper

For the Sousing Liquid

2 teaspoons olive oil
½ onion, roughly chopped
1 small carrot, roughly chopped
1 celery stalk, roughly chopped
1 sprig of fresh thyme
1 sprig of fresh tarragon
1 bay leaf

1 star anise (optional)
2 teaspoons pickling spice
⅓ cup white wine
⅓ cup white wine vinegar
2 cups water
A pinch of salt
Juice of ½ lemon

Pre-heat the oven to 375°F (190°C).

Roll out the pastry very thinly, cut into 3-4 inch (7.5-10 cm) discs and leave to rest in the refrigerator for 20 minutes. Bake in the pre-heated oven for about 10 minutes until cooked through and crisp.

To caramelize the onions, simply place them in a pan with a tablespoon of water and cook, uncovered, over a low heat for about 2 hours until all the natural juices and sugars from the onions begin to color to a rich, golden brown. This can be done in advance.

Cook the red peppers in the olive oil for 2-3 minutes until softened. Add to the caramelized onions and season with salt and pepper.

Meanwhile, make the sousing liquid. Warm the olive oil and add the onion, carrot, celery, thyme, tarragon, bay leaf, star anise and pickling spice. Cook for a few minutes until the vegetables begin to soften. Add the white wine, wine vinegar and water with a pinch of salt and the lemon juice. Bring to the simmer and cook for 15-20 minutes. Strain.

Place the mackerel fillets in the warm sousing liquid and bring almost to the simmer. This will just warm them through, keeping the fish succulent and juicy.

Sweeten the dressing with a little balsamic vinegar and add the chives.

Spoon the warm onion and pepper mix onto the pastry discs and lay the mackerel fillets on top. Spoon the dressing over and around the mackerel.

Variations

If you haven't got enough time to make the caramelized onions, simply fry 2 or 3 sliced onions in butter until golden brown and almost burnt. This will give a more bittersweet taste that will become a lot sweeter when added to the red pepper.

*Fillet of Mackerel with Caramelized Onions
and Sweet Peppers.*

Broiled Mackerel with Mussel Stew

You can leave out the first stage in cooking the mussel stew if you wish and simply cook the mussels in fish stock, but the pre-cooking does give a lot more flavor to the cooking liquid. Turn to p.30 for the finished dish.

SERVES 4

4 mackerel fillets
2 tablespoons unsalted butter

Salt and freshly ground black pepper

For the Mussel Cooking Liquid

1 tablespoon unsalted butter
1 carrot, diced
1 onion, diced
1 celery stalk, diced
1 bay leaf

1 sprig of fresh tarragon
1¼ cups dry white wine
2½ cups Fish Stock (see p.221)
2 lb (900 g) fresh mussels, washed and
   bearded

For the Stew

2 tablespoons olive oil
½ cup (8 tablespoons) unsalted butter
2 large carrots, cut into ¼ inch (5 mm)
   dice
2 onions, cut into ¼ inch (5 mm) dice
3 celery stalks, cut into ¼ inch (5 mm) dice
1 bouquet garni (a few fresh basil and
   tarragon leaves and 1 star anise tied
   in a muslin bag)

1¼ cups dry white wine
2 teaspoons Pesto Sauce (see p.235)
2 large tomatoes, skinned, seeded and
   diced
1 teaspoon chopped fresh parsley

Butter and season a baking sheet.

Trim the mackerel fillets and remove all central bones. This can be done easily by cutting either side of the bones down to the skin but not cutting through. Pick from the head and pull out the central bones; they will come away from the skin in one piece. Place the fillets on the prepared baking sheet skin-side-up. Brush the skin with butter and season with salt and pepper, then place in the refrigerator.

To cook the mussel liquid, melt the butter in a pan and add the carrot, onion, celery, bay leaf and tarragon and cook gently, without coloring, until softened. Add the white wine and boil until the liquid has almost evaporated. Add the stock and bring to a rapid simmer.

To clean the mussels, run under cold water and scrape until all grit and beard are removed. Discard any that are open and do not close when tapped sharply. Drain from the water and drop into the cooking liquid. Bring back to the boil, stirring frequently. As soon as the mussels begin to open, drain in a colander, reserving the stock. This should now be drained through a fine sieve. Pick the mussels from their shells and check that they are clean from all impurities. Discard any that have not opened.

Warm a pan and add the olive oil and 2 tablespoons of the butter. Add the diced vegetables with the bouquet garni. Cook without coloring until they begin to soften. Add the white wine and reduce until almost dry. Add enough of the mussel stock until the vegetables are covered; you may not need all of the stock so just add a little at a time. Bring to a simmer and cook until the vegetables are tender. This will take about 8-10 minutes.

Pre-heat the broiler.

Cook the mackerel fillets under the pre-heated broiler until the skin is crisp. The fish will only take between 4-6 minutes.

While the mackerel is cooking, whisk the remaining butter into the liquid and add some pesto sauce to taste, the diced tomatoes, chopped fresh parsley and, of course, the mussels. Warm through and spoon into large bowls, distributing the garnish equally. Sit the mackerel on top and serve.

ABOVE *Broiled Mackerel with Mussel Stew (see p.28).*

RIGHT *Seared Peppered Salmon (see p.32) and
Cucumber Pickle (see p.244).*

Seared Peppered Salmon

This dish has very few ingredients but the method and preparation give lots of texture and taste. It's like eating warm salmon gravlax with a fiery bite from the pepper.

The salmon can just be sliced and eaten, but the raw black pepper is very strong. The purpose of the searing is to take away that rawness, create texture and give aroma and bite. I like to eat it with Cucumber Pickle (see p.244) – classic salmon and cucumber combination with a difference!

SERVES 4-6

1 lb (450 g) salmon fillet with skin	1 tablespoon sugar
1 tablespoon finely ground black pepper	Olive oil
1 tablespoon salt	Lemon or lime juice

Trim the salmon fillet and remove any bones. Along the fillet run several "pin" bones; these can easily be removed with tweezers or small pliers. The black pepper must be finely ground. You can do this in a food processor or in a pepper mill. Shake the pepper through a sieve to leave you with a fine grind. Mix with the salt and sugar and sprinkle over the salmon so that it is covered in one layer of ground black pepper. Wrap the salmon in plastic wrap and chill. The salmon will be "cooked" by the salt and sugar mix. This curing process can take as little as 1-2 hours, but I like to make this in the morning for eating in the evening.

Remove the plastic wrap and cut the salmon into ¾-1¼ inch (2-3 cm) thick slices. Pre-heat a frying pan and brush with olive oil. Make sure the pan is hot. Sit the salmon in the pan and sear for about 15-20 seconds on one side. Providing that the pan is hot, the salmon will be almost raw but just colored, with very slightly burnt tinges burnt on the pepper. Serve the salmon as a starter with a squeeze of lemon or lime juice or try it sitting on the Cucumber Pickle.

Smoked Salmon and Asparagus with Poached Egg Hollandaise

Cold smoked salmon on warm toast with warm asparagus and a gently poached egg just breaking on top sounds delicious – and it is. Lots of traditional flavors working together. This dish can be even better. I like to top the poached egg with Hollandaise Sauce (see p.235). It eats beautifully and gives a good finish to the dish.

SERVES 4

12-16 medium asparagus spears	Horseradish sauce or cream
Salt	8 oz (225 g) sliced smoked salmon
2 tablespoons unsalted butter	4 poached eggs
4 thick slices wholewheat bread	1 recipe Hollandaise Sauce (see p.235)

The first job is to prepare and cook the asparagus. To be certain of them being tender, lightly peel them from half way down to the base of the spears and cut about 1 inch (2.5 cm) off the root. The asparagus will now be deep green from the top, changing tones down to white.

Drop the asparagus into boiling salted water and keep on full heat for 2-3 minutes, then drain. The spears will still have a nice bite in them. If you are cooking the asparagus in advance, simply drop them into ice cold water to refresh them. To re-heat, just drop them back into hot water for 30-40 seconds, lift out, season with salt and pepper and brush with butter.

Toast the bread and spread with a thin layer of horseradish sauce or cream; the flavor works really well with smoked salmon. Cover the toast with the salmon and the asparagus tips on top. Sit the warm poached eggs on top and finish with hollandaise sauce.

Variations

Instead of the hollandaise, you can use some Basic Vinaigrette (see p.241) with snipped fresh chives and just spoon it over the egg.

Grilled Tuna with Salsa Dressing
or Sauerkraut

As you can see in the title, there are already two options for the tuna in this recipe, both of which are excellent. This dish also eats well as a main course. The tuna is best cooked and served as a medium rare steak, still nice and pink in the center, to help the taste and texture. The tuna can be grilled or pan-fried, and should be served warm with the cold salsa dressing (p.243) or with the warm sauerkraut.

If fresh tuna is unavailable, then other fish can be used - salmon, red mullet, trout or more. Canned tuna can also be used and broken down with a fork and then mixed with the salsa dressing; this eats very well with a salad or even just a sandwich filling. The sauerkraut will only really work with fresh tuna steaks. The sauerkraut version is best served warm on the plate topped with some salad leaves and then the tuna steak sat on top. A good basic dressing with chopped chives goes very well with this dish.

The salsa is best served just sat next to the tuna with some green leaves (see p.10).

SERVES 4-6

4 (4–6 oz) (100–175 g) tuna fillet steaks	Basic Vinaigrette (see p.241)
Olive oil	Salsa Dressing (see p.243)
Salt and freshly ground black pepper	OR
Green or mixed salad leaves	½ recipe Sauerkraut (see p.94)

To cook the tuna, lightly brush the fish with olive oil and season with salt and pepper. The fish can now either be grilled on a hot ridged grill pan or barbecue or pan-fried in a hot frying pan. If the thickness of the steaks is ½ inch (1 cm) the fish will only take 1-2 minutes on each side before it is ready to serve.

Toss the salad leaves in a little vinaigrette and arrange on plates with the steak.

Now all you have to do is decide – salsa or sauerkraut!

Grilling the tuna steak.

Crab and Salmon Fritters

These are a wonderful savory starter that can also be cooked for hot canapés. The crab and salmon go together very well but both could be substituted with chopped prawns and cod or lots of other combinations. Once cooked until golden and crispy, I like to serve them with a sour cream lemon or lime dip made by flavoring some sour cream with lemon or lime juice, salt and pepper. This recipe comes in two parts: the crab and salmon filling and the choux pastry to bind it.

SERVES 6–8

For the Pastry

⅔ cup water
4 tablespoons butter
1 cup all-purpose flour

2 eggs, beaten
A pinch of salt

For the Filling

8 oz (225 g) salmon fillet
Salt and freshly ground white pepper
¾ cup white wine
1 tablespoon unsalted butter
2 teaspoons olive oil
1 green bell pepper, finely diced

1 red bell pepper, finely diced
½ bunch green onions, finely diced
1½ tablespoons ginger root, finely grated
8 oz (225 g) cooked white crab meat
1 teaspoon chopped fresh dill
Tabasco sauce
Oil for deep-frying

Pre-heat the oven to 400°F (200°C) and grease and season a baking sheet with salt and pepper.

To make the pastry, bring the water and butter to the boil. Remove from the heat and add the flour. Return the pan to a moderate heat and cook, stirring vigorously, until the paste comes away from the sides of the pan. Leave to cool. Gradually beat the eggs into the dough with the salt, leaving you with a smooth choux pastry mix with a dropping consistency.

To cook the salmon, sit it in the baking pan and add the white wine. Cover with foil and bake in the pre-heated oven for 10–15 minutes, depending on the thickness of the fish. To check the salmon, it should be just firm to the touch, cooked like a medium steak, still pink in the middle. Once cooked, allow to cool. Reserve any cooking liquid.

Melt the butter with the olive oil. When it begins to bubble, add the peppers, green onions and ginger and cook for 1–2 minutes. Remove from the pan and allow to cool.

The crab meat can be bought cooked and prepared (it's also possible to buy it frozen). Break it down and checked through for any broken shell. Add the salmon, peppers and dill and season with salt, pepper and a few drops of Tabasco sauce. Bind together with the choux pastry.

Heat the deep-frying oil to 350°F (180°C). Spoon the fritter mix straight from the bowl into the fryer or on to a floured pan before cooking. This gives a rustic natural shape. Fry the fritters until golden brown and crispy. If they seem to be cooking too quickly, then turn the fryer down to 300°F (150°C).

Note

The fritters should be no bigger than a soup spoon size. This will ensure they cook evenly. For little tasters, the size of a teaspoon should be just right.

Crumbled Baked Sardine Fillets

This dish can only really be made with fresh sardines. Sardines are great for grilling whole on a barbecue or under the broiler, but the small bones can often be too much hard work. So for this dish, ask your fishmonger to scale and fillet them for you. If they are from large sardines you will only need three or four fillets a portion as a starter. Some of the small bones within the fillets can be removed with a small knife or tweezers. Any remaining ones are quite edible as for canned sardines. The "crumbled" is a breadcrumb and fresh herb mix sprinkled on top and broiled. Once crumbled, the sardines can be served on a simple salad or just with a squeeze of lemon.

SERVES 4

6–8 sardines, filleted	Olive oil
Mixed green salad leaves	A few drops of lemon juice

For the Crumble Topping

2 tablespoons unsalted butter	1 teaspoon chopped fresh parsley
1 large shallot or ½ onion, finely chopped	½ teaspoon chopped fresh tarragon
	½ teaspoon chopped fresh basil
4 slices white bread, crusts removed and crumbed	Salt and freshly ground white pepper
	Juice of ½ lemon

For the Anchovy Dip

6 canned anchovy fillets, drained	Juice of 1 lemon
1 egg	½ teaspoon chopped fresh thyme
2 tablespoons capers	A pinch of sugar
1 garlic clove, crushed	¼ cup warm water
1 inch (2.5 cm) ginger root, peeled and chopped	Scant 1 cup olive oil
1 bunch of fresh basil leaves	Scant 1 cup peanut oil

Pre-heat the broiler and butter and season a baking sheet with salt and pepper.

To make the crumble topping, melt the butter with the chopped shallot or onion and cook without coloring for 1-2 minutes. Mix the breadcrumbs and chopped herbs and season with salt and pepper. Mix some of the shallot butter into the crumbs until a crumbly texture is formed; you may not need all the shallot mixture. Add a few drops of lemon juice to the mix.

Sit the sardine fillets skin-side-up on the baking sheet. Sprinkle the crumble crumbs on top of each fillet. Place the sardines under a hot broiler. Once the crumbs have become golden brown and crispy the fillets will be cooked; it will take just a few minutes.

Meanwhile, to make the anchovy dip, place all the ingredients, except the oils, in a food processor and purée to a paste. With the processor still running, slowly add the oil as you would for mayonnaise. Season the dressing with salt and pepper and push through a fine sieve. The dressing will have a mayonnaise sauce consistency with a hint of green from the basil and capers.

Toss the salad leaves in some olive oil with salt and pepper and a few drops of lemon juice.

Spoon the anchovy dip onto the plates, forming a circular pattern. Sit the salad leaves on the center of the sauce and place the crumbled fillets on top of the lettuce. The dish is ready!

Grilled King Prawns with Warm Spicy Relish

This dish is great as a starter or main course. King prawns can be cooked loose or made into kebabs (about five prawns per portion as a main course, or three or four as a starter) and cook really well on the open gas grill or barbecue. That's the beauty of a dish like this: it has so many combinations and options. The prawns taste delicious with the spicy relish, or you can just serve them on their own, with a squeeze of lemon or with mayonnaise. Also, you don't have to use king prawns. Just ordinary fresh prawns (or even frozen!) will also eat really well with the warm relish. You can eat the whole lot cold, warm under the broiler or toss in butter in a frying pan. That's how simple and easy this dish can be.

This relish can be made several days in advance and kept chilled, then either served cold or simply re-heated. Oh, and by the way, the relish also eats well with other fish and also chicken, so have a go!

To save time, you can use a can of chopped tomatoes for this recipe; it's never quite the same but it does work. You can simply drain off all liquid from the can and add the tomatoes to the mix, or you can boil the tomatoes to reduce all the excess liquid until thick and strong in flavor before adding this to the mixture.

SERVES 4-6

20 raw king prawns	Salt and freshly ground black pepper
Olive oil	

For the Tomato Relish

8 plum tomatoes	2 fresh green chilies, very finely diced
1 tablespoon olive oil	1 teaspoon tomato paste
2 large red onions, finely chopped	2 teaspoons demerara or light brown
1 garlic clove, crushed	sugar
2 green bell peppers, seeded and finely	1½ tablespoons malt vinegar
diced	Salt

Pre-heat a gas grill or barbecue.

If the prawns are whole including heads, then first remove the heads, then pick the shell from the tails, leaving the base of tail intact. The prawns can be placed on wooden skewers or left loose. Brush the prawns with olive oil and season with salt and pepper.

The prawns will take about 1½-2 minutes per side on a hot open gas grill or barbecue, under a domestic oven broiler or in a frying pan.

To make the relish, remove the cores from the tomatoes, then blanch them in boiling water for 8-10 seconds, then refresh in cold water and remove the skins. Quarter the tomatoes and remove all the seeds and water. Dice the flesh into ¼ inch (5 mm) dice.

Warm the olive oil in a pan and cook the chopped red onions over a low heat for a few minutes until they begin to soften. Add the garlic, peppers and chilies, increasing the heat to medium. Continue to cook for a few minutes. Add the tomatoes and tomato paste and cook for about 6-8 minutes. As the tomatoes cook, all excess water will be released, creating a tomato sauce effect. However, this may seem a little too thin, so either continue to cook until a thicker tomato base is achieved or, and I think this is better, simply drain off all juices through a sieve and simmer the liquid on the stove until it begins to thicken, then remix with the other ingredients. You will now have a tasty warm chili relish. To finish it off and give a spicy effect, mix together the demerara or light brown sugar and malt vinegar and bring to the boil. This mix will only take a couple of minutes to boil and reduce in volume. The consistency should be like a thick syrup. Add this to the relish a little at a time, tasting until a sweet and sour flavor is achieved. Season with salt and pepper.

Variations

If you are using small, frozen peeled prawns, then why not mix some cold spicy relish with mayonnaise and turn the whole dish into a spicy prawn cocktail?

Griddled Scallops with Crispy Eggplant

This dish shows another taste alternative with basic ingredients. The sweetness of the scallops mixed with an almost bitter/burnt flavor of the frying works really well with the tomato and olive taste. For a quick salad dressing, just mix a few drops of balsamic vinegar with some olive oil and season with salt and pepper. Alternatively, a good extra-virgin olive oil would be enough on its own. Turn to p.11 to see the finished dish.

Serves 4

1 large eggplant
2–3 tablespoons all-purpose flour
1 teaspoon cayenne pepper
Salt and freshly ground white pepper
Oil for deep-frying
1 recipe Tomato Relish (see p.40)

6–8 black olives, finely diced
Basic Vinaigrette (see p.241) or olive oil
2 tablespoons unsalted butter
12 large scallops, cleaned and trimmed
Mixed green salad leaves such as
    arugula, curly endive, baby spinach

Split the eggplant lengthwise and slice across thinly. Mix the all-purpose flour with the cayenne pepper and a pinch of salt. Sprinkle the flour over the eggplant and lightly dust off any excess. These can now be fried in hot oil until golden and crispy. Drain off any excess fat and sprinkle with salt. The eggplant can be cooked before cooking the scallops and will stay crispy and warm before finishing the dish.

Warm the tomato relish, then mix the chopped black olives with a little vinaigrette or olive oil.

Heat a frying pan until very hot but not burning, add a few drops of olive oil and a little butter. Sit the scallops in the pan, in batches if necessary, keeping the pan hot. If the pan is not hot enough, the scallops will simply begin to stew in their own juices which will spoil their taste and texture. Once they have colored golden brown on both sides, turn them out, season with salt and pepper and repeat the same process if you are cooking in batches. This will only take 2–3 minutes.

Season the salad leaves and toss with a little olive oil. Spoon the warm tomato relish into the center of the plate, making a circular platform for the scallops. Spoon the black olive dressing around. Sit the scallops on to the relish and place the salad leaves in the center. To finish the dish, simply arrange the fried eggplant on top.

*Spooning the black olives around the tomato relish
while the scallops cook on the griddle.*

Fried Cockle Salad

Eating deep-fried cockles is delicious. They get really crispy and tasty. Just be careful not to fry too many at once otherwise you'll almost have a popcorn situation. So it's best to use a deep-fat fryer, or certainly a large pan with a lid.

The crispy cockles eat very well with Salsa Dressing (see p.243), although it is best to make the relish looser with more olive oil and lime juice, making it into more of a dressing.

You can buy cooked cockles in most fishmongers and supermarkets. If you buy live cockles, wash them well, removing any grit, then drop them into a pan of boiling water. The cockles will start to open after 30 seconds. Once they are open, drain off the water and leave the cockles to cool. Pick the cockles from their shells and leave to drain on a cloth. If you can't find cockles, try Manila clams.

Use whichever salad leaves you prefer. There's plenty of choice, from red oak leaf and curly endive to arugula.

SERVES 4

1 recipe Salsa Dressing (see p.243)	6-8 oz (175-225 g) fresh cooked cockles
2-3 tablespoons olive oil	or Manila clams
Juice of ½ lime	2-3 tablespoons milk
Salt and freshly ground white pepper	2-3 tablespoons self-rising flour
Oil for deep-frying	Mixed salad leaves

Loosen the salsa relish recipe with some more olive oil and a few drops of extra lime juice. Check the dressing for seasoning with salt and pepper.

To cook the cockles, remove from the shells, pre-heat the fat fryer to 350°F (180°C). Coat the cockles in milk, then roll lightly through the flour, shaking off any excess. Fry the cockles in the pre-heated oil for 1-2 minutes until golden and crispy. Lift them from the fryer and sprinkle with salt.

Spoon the relish onto the plates and scatter over the crispy cockles. Mix the salad leaves with a few drops of olive oil and season with salt and pepper. Sit the leaves in a small pile in the center of the plate. The leaves should be standing high with the dressing and cockles being visible all around the plate.

Sautéed Scallop and Fennel Salad

Scallops are available fresh from many fishmongers, or you may find some good quality scallops frozen.

SERVES 4

4 fennel bulbs
Juice of 1 lemon
1 star anise (optional)
3¾ cups water
Salt and freshly ground white pepper
4-6 tablespoons unsalted butter

1 tablespoon olive oil
12 scallops, trimmed and roes removed
Green salad leaves
Basic Vinaigrette (see p.241)
1 tablespoon snipped fresh chives

Top and tail the fennel. Using a small knife, remove the core from the base of each fennel. Add the lemon juice and star anise to the water with a pinch of salt and bring to the boil. Add the fennel, cover and simmer over a medium heat for 15-20 minutes until just tender.

Pour off half of the cooking liquid and boil it to reduce to about ⅔ cup. This will increase the flavor of the fennel. Add the butter to the liquid and whisk vigorously to make a butter sauce. For an even lighter and smoother sauce, use a food processor or electric blender to finish. This sauce can be kept warm and re-heated and puréed before serving.

Slice the fennel ¼ inch (5 mm) thick lengthwise. Heat a frying pan and add a teaspoon of olive oil to the pan. Fry the fennel slices on both sides until golden brown. Season with salt and pepper.

To cook the scallops, heat a frying pan with a few drops of olive oil and a tablespoon of butter. It is very important to cook scallops in a hot pan. This will color and seal them quickly. If the pan is only warm, the scallops will begin to poach in their own juices, creating a different texture and taste. Once colored and seasoned on both sides, the scallops are ready; this should only take 2-3 minutes depending on size.

To serve the dish, lay the fennel slices on the center of a warmed serving plate and sit the scallops on top. Mix the salad leaves with a little vinaigrette and sit them in the center of the scallops. Add the chives to the sauce and spoon around the plate.

Warm Smoked Eel and Fava Bean Broth on Mashed Potatoes

Smoked eel has a wonderful flavor. It's really good to use in a stew or simply cold with a horseradish sauce. The combination of flavors in this dish can work well together either for a cold or hot dish. This is a tasty hot version.

SERVES 4

1–1½ lb (450–675 g) smoked eel

For the Stock

1 onion, chopped
1 leek, chopped
2 celery stalks, chopped
1 bay leaf
1 cup mushroom trimmings (optional)
1 sprig of fresh thyme

2 sprigs of fresh tarragon
A few black peppercorns
2 tablespoons unsalted butter
1¼ cups white wine
3¾ cups Fish Stock (see p.221) or water

To Finish

1½ cups or ¼ recipe Mashed Potatoes
  (see p.133)
1 tablespoon finely chopped shallots
Juice of 1½ lemons
Salt and freshly ground black pepper

½ cup (8 tablespoons) unsalted butter
10 oz (300 g) fava beans, cooked and
  shelled
1 tablespoon snipped fresh chives

Fillet and skin the smoked eel, saving all the trimmings for the stock. Hopefully, your fishmonger will do this for you, but if not, simply cut off the head and position the knife against the top half of the central bone. Carefully cut along the bone, removing the fillet of fish. Turn the fish over and repeat the same process. Now the skin can be removed. Slide your finger or thumb under the skin at the head end and it should tear off all the way along. The fillets may need a little trimming down the sides to remove any excess skin. Turn the fillets on their back to show the center. From the head end to halfway down there will be some bones. Simply position the knife under these bones and cut away from the flesh. You now have two long, clean fillets of eel. Cut these into diagonal 1 inch (2.5 cm) pieces and keep in the refrigerator.

To make the stock, place the chopped vegetables, herbs and peppercorns in a pan with the butter and cook without coloring for 10 minutes. Add the chopped eel bones and trimmings and continue to cook for 5 minutes. Add the white wine and boil to reduce until almost dry. Add the stock or water. If you are using water ask your fishmonger to give you some fish bones to cook with the eel trimmings. Bring the stock to the simmer and cook for 20 minutes. Strain through a sieve. Re-boil the eel stock and reduce to 2-2½ cups to increase the eel flavor.

Re-heat 1¼ cups of reduced eel stock. Warm the mashed potatoes, add the raw chopped shallot and juice of 1 lemon and season with salt and pepper. Add the butter to the eel stock and whisk into a light frothy broth; a hand blender can be used to help this. Add the fava beans and warm through. Drop the pieces of smoked eel into the liquid with the remaining lemon juice and the chives and continue to warm. Spoon or pipe the mashed potatoes into the center of a bowl or plate and spoon over the eel and fava bean broth.

Fillets of Smoked Eel on a Warm Potato, Onion and Beet Salad

The potato, beet and onion salad eats very well with the smoked eel. This dressing also tastes good with the addition of 2 teaspoons of horseradish, but I'm keeping this fairly simple to make.

SERVES 4

1 smoked eel, filleted and skinned (see p.46)
8 oz (225 g) new potatoes, cooked
½ – ¾ cup Basic Vinaigrette (see p.241)
1 cup caramelized onion (see p.26)

1 large cooked beet
Salt and freshly ground black pepper
1 tablespoon chopped fresh parsley
Mixed salad leaves, such as arugula, baby spinach, curly endive

Cut the smoked eel into 2-3 inch (5-7.5 cm) slices, allowing three or four slices per portion. While the new potatoes are still warm, leave the skin on and cut them in half. Add three-quarters of the dressing and the cooked onions and continue to warm in the pan. Add the beet, making sure that it's carefully mixed in and not coloring all the potatoes. Check for seasoning with salt and pepper. Add the chopped fresh parsley. Season the remaining dressing and add to the salad leaves. Divide the potato and beet salad between four plates. Sit the leaves on top of the salads and lay the smoked eel on top. Finish with the chopped fresh parsley dressing.

Smoked Eel and Fava Bean Salad

This is as simple as it sounds – very few ingredients but plenty of taste. It is a very basic salad that can take on so many more flavors. Sliced, cooked, peeled new potatoes can be warmed in the horseradish or mustard dressing and placed underneath the salad, and a hot poached egg can be popped on the top before finishing with the fava beans. Breaking the egg yolk over the smoked eel and salad and mixing it with warm new potatoes in a horseradish and mustard dressing – delicious!

SERVES 4

1 lb (450 g) smoked eel fillet, cut into 3 inch (7.5 cm) strips
⅔ cup Basic Vinaigrette (see p.241)
Juice of ½ lemon
Salt and freshly ground black pepper

1 teaspoon horseradish sauce or stone-ground mustard
10 oz (275 g) cooked and shelled fava beans
Mixed salad leaves

The smoked eel should be at room temperature. Mix 1 tablespoon of vinaigrette with a few drops of lemon juice and re-season with salt and pepper. This dressing will be used to flavor the salad leaves.

Warm the remaining dressing and flavor with the horseradish sauce or stone-ground mustard. Both flavors work well with smoked eel. Add the fava beans to the dressing and warm through. Toss the salad leaves in the salad dressing with salt and pepper and arrange the leaves on plates. Sit the smoked eel fingers on top of the salad, slightly overlapping. Spoon the fava bean dressing over the eels and serve.

Note

Fava beans should be cooked in boiling, salted water until tender. This can take 6-12 minutes depending on the size of the bean. Refresh under ice water and shell. The beans will have a rich, deep green color and can be kept in the refrigerator and used when required.

Chicken Wing Salad

If you have chicken wings left after preparing chicken breasts, this is a great way to use them. Barbecued chicken wings make a quick and easy snack, salad or lunch dish.

SERVES 4

2 lb (900 g) chicken wings	2 tablespoons soy sauce
1 tablespoon paprika	Olive or cooking oil
Juice of 1-2 lemons	Mixed salad leaves

Dust the chicken wings lightly with paprika. Add the lemon juice and soy sauce and toss together well. You can cook the wings now, but I prefer to leave them to take on the taste for anything from a few hours to a few days.

Lift the wings from the marinade. The best way to cook the wings is on an open barbecue. If you cannot do this, pre-heat the oven to 425°F (220°C). Pre-heat a roasting pan on top of the stove with a little olive or cooking oil. Fry the wings until well colored (even with a few burnt tinges), then transfer to the oven for 10-15 minutes.

Once the wings are cooked, pour over the marinade and bring to the boil. Remove from the heat and stir well. This will give the wings a paprika, lemon and soy glaze. Serve the wings on top of a mixed salad as a starter or in a big bowl for everyone to help themselves.

Variations

The wings also eat well with sour cream as a dip.

Spicy chicken wings for the Chicken Wing Salad.

Niçoise Salad

This country-style salad starter has over the years almost become a chefs' "designer salad." The tomatoes are laid at 12 o'clock, 3 o'clock, 6 o'oclock and 9 o'clock and all the other flavors follow suit at 10 minutes to and 10 minutes past! Chefs could argue all day over what should be included. Should there be tuna or anchovies or both?

Well, I'm going to give you my version, with the first five ingredients coming from the original recipe and the rest the optional extras. I include tuna fish, but it's going to be broiled fresh tuna fillet to sit on top of the finished salad. Of course this can be left out of the recipe completely or replaced with broken tuna fish tossed into the salad.

SERVES 4

12 very thin slices French bread	1 teaspoon small capers
4 tablespoons olive oil or garlic butter	4 oz (100 g) French green beans, crisply cooked
1 head of soft lettuce or mixed salad leaves	4–8 canned or marinated anchovy fillets
8 black olives, pitted and quartered	8 new potatoes, cooked and sliced
2 plum tomatoes, seeded and cut into 6-8 wedges	Salt and freshly ground black pepper
	4 (4 oz) (100 g) tuna fillet steaks

For the Dressing

6-8 tablespoons olive oil	½ small garlic clove, finely crushed
2 tablespoons tarragon vinegar	½ teaspoon snipped fresh chives
½ teaspoon Dijon mustard	½ teaspoon chopped fresh tarragon
Freshly ground peppercorns	2 hard-boiled eggs, roughly chopped
A pinch of salt	

To make the dressing, simply mix all the ingredients except the herbs and eggs in a jar or bottle, only adding the fresh herbs just before finishing the salad. If the herbs are added too early the tarragon vinegar will discolor them.

Brush the bread with olive oil or garlic butter. Toast until golden and crisp on both sides. Separate the salad leaves and add the olives, tomatoes, capers, French green beans and anchovy fillets. Add the potato slices and season with salt and pepper.

Season the tuna with salt and pepper and start to broil or shallow-fry for about 1-1½ minutes on each side, keeping the tuna medium rare to medium.

While the tuna fish is cooking, mix the salad dressing with the chopped herbs and chopped hard-boiled egg. Pour some over the salad and toss together with the toasts. Divide between plates and sit the tuna on top.

Raw Fennel Salad

Fennel is a vegetable that is not used enough. It has the most wonderful anise flavor and can be eaten raw or cooked. To eat raw fennel, slice it very thinly, otherwise it will be tough. All it needs then is a good marinade or dressing in which it should be served chilled. Eating a good, cold fennel salad with dressing is so refreshing and works all your taste buds. This can be eaten as a side dish to go with fish, or on its own.

Cooked fennel has many uses in salads, fish and meat dishes, or as a vegetable. It can also be served just with a dressing or broiled or shallow-fried with sauces and spices. I like it with hot Griddled Scallops (see p.42), Seared Peppered Salmon (see p.32) or grilled fresh tuna cooked on a barbecue or hot ridged grill pan.

Serves 4

| 2 fennel bulbs | Juice of 2 lemons |
| 7 tablespoons olive oil | Salt and freshly ground white pepper |

Trim the root and tops of the fennel and slice on a machine or cut very thinly with a sharp knife into rings. Mix together the olive oil and lemon juice and season with salt and pepper. Add to the fennel rings. The fennel will now taste crunchy with an acidic taste of lemon and rich olive oil.

Variations

It's also nice to turn this recipe into a full starter served with a tarragon mayonnaise. Just add chopped fresh tarragon and a few drops of tarragon vinegar to Mayonnaise (see p.242). Spoon the sauce into a bowl and sit some salad leaves on top, finishing with the fennel.

Caesar Salad

This salad was a great invention. You'll notice that the egg should only be boiled for 1½ minutes. This helps the binding of the dressing without the whites being totally raw. If you are still worried about this, then simply use the yolk from one or two hard-boiled eggs; the dressing will still work. Tabasco sauce is very hot and strong, so a dash must literally be just one or two drops. Marinated anchovy fillets are bought soaked in a vinegar liquid, making them packed with flavor and taste.

SERVES 4

For the Salad

2 heads of romaine	Olive oil
12 marinated or 8 canned anchovy fillets	¼ cup Parmesan, grated
4 thick slices wholewheat bread	½ cup Parmesan flakes

For the Dressing

½ oz (15 g) anchovy fillets, drained and chopped	½ garlic clove, crushed
2 teaspoons capers	2 tablespoons finely grated Parmesan
2 teaspoons Worcestershire sauce	1 egg, boiled for 1½ minutes only
½ teaspoon Dijon mustard	⅔-1¼ cups extra-virgin olive oil
A dash of Tabasco sauce	Freshly ground black pepper
Juice of ½ lemon	

Break down the lettuces into separate leaves. Split the anchovy fillets into strips. Remove the crusts from the bread and cut into ½ inch (1 cm) squares. These can be shallow-fried, toasted or (and this is what I do!) sprinkled with olive oil and baked in a pre-heated oven at 400°F (200°C). Keep turning them every minute or so until golden brown and crunchy. Cooking them this way prevents them from becoming soaked in oil. While still hot, toss them in the grated Parmesan.

The quickest way to make the dressing is to place all the ingredients in a blender, using just ⅔ cup of oil to start with, and purée until thick and creamy. Check for seasoning. Be careful of using any salt in this dressing because of the high salt content of the anchovies. The dressing can be pushed through a sieve or left rustic, which will give you more texture. If necessary, you can add a little more oil at a time. The consistency should be thick and emulsified, coating the back of a spoon.

To assemble the salad, toss the Romaine leaves in the dressing, making sure they are all coated. Add the anchovies, croûtons and half of the Parmesan flakes and divide between the salad bowls. Sprinkle with the remaining Parmesan.

Caesar Salad.

Risotto

Risotto is a specialty rice dish from northern Italy and there is no other rice dish quite like it. The best rice all round to use (and only for this dish really) is arborio. This is an almost round rice that has an outer layer that creates a wonderful creamy texture as it cooks. It's the cooking method that creates this consistency: just adding a little stock at a time which, as it's braising on top of the stove, starts to break down the layers.

Risotto can be as basic and easy or as exciting and difficult as you wish. Probably the classic Italian risotto is Milanese, which is made with saffron and Parmesan; quite a simple dish that sparked off many variations.

All my risotto recipes are flexible; you can change the ingredients to suit yourself. One ingredient that is used in many Italian risottos is beef bone marrow. Added to the onions while they are softening in the butter and olive oil, this adds a richness to the dish which lifts the flavor and texture. It can be used in any of these risottos just adding 1-2 oz (25-50 g) per recipe. Risottos can also be lovely vegetarian dishes, providing vegetable stock is used.

Here are the basic quantities for any risotto – the proportions of rice, stock, onions and butter are the same – a simple blueprint for making up your own.

1½ cups arborio rice
5 cups Vegetable Stock (see p.223),
   Chicken Stock (see p.222) or Fish
   stock (see p.221)

½-¾ cup (8-12 tablespoons) unsalted
   butter
2 onions, finely chopped

Finely grated Parmesan added at the end of cooking enriches all the flavors and makes the consistency even more creamy.

Mushroom Risotto with Crispy Black Pudding Sausage

Mushrooms and black pudding sausage are a traditional British combination, usually served at breakfast. They work together very well in this recipe, contrasting the creaminess of the risotto with the crispy, rich black sausage. The best mushrooms to use in this recipe are Portobello. These have an almost meaty texture and a much better flavor, but if you can't find them, any mushroom will do.

SERVES 4-8

8-12 tablespoons unsalted butter
1 tablespoon olive oil
2 onions, finely chopped
1-2 oz (25-50 g) bone marrow, chopped (optional)
5 cups Vegetable Stock (see p.223) or Chicken Stock (see p.222)
8-12 oz (225-350 g) Portobello

mushrooms, sliced
1¼ cups arborio rice
12 oz (350 g) black pudding sausage or pork sausage, cut into ½ inch (1 cm) dice
1-2 tablespoons freshly grated Parmesan
Salt and freshly ground black pepper
Parmesan flakes

Melt the butter with the olive oil in a large pan. Add the chopped onion and chopped bone marrow, if using, and cook without coloring for 2-3 minutes. Meanwhile, bring the stock to the boil. Add the sliced mushrooms to the onions, increasing the heat of the pan. Allow the mushrooms to cook for 2-3 minutes. Add the rice and continue to cook over a medium heat for a further minute. Add the hot stock a ladle at a time, allowing it to become absorbed in the rice and evaporate before adding another ladle. Continue this process, stirring almost continuously to keep an even cooking. This will take 20-30 minutes. When the risotto is almost cooked, the black pudding sausage can be either pan-fried until crispy or cooked under the broiler.

Once the risotto is cooked, add some grated Parmesan and check the consistency is of a rich creamy texture. Season with salt and pepper and spoon on to a plate or into bowls. Sprinkle with fresh Parmesan flakes, crispy black pudding sausage and a few drops of olive oil.

ABOVE *Crab Risotto (see p.60).*
OPPOSITE *Checking the flavor of the risotto.*

Crab Risotto

Seafood risottos are really delightful to eat. In Italy, meat or fish are always included in the dish rather than served with it, making the risotto a complete meal in itself (see p.58).

For the maximum crab flavor, it's best to use fresh crab cooked in fish stock. This will leave you with a good crab stock to lift the flavor. If you are using fresh crab, follow the cooking method from the bisque recipe on p.16. Otherwise cooked white crab meat can be obtained from most fishmongers or supermarkets, either fresh or frozen.

I also like to serve the risotto finished with a border of crab bisque (see Lobster Bisque p.16). This is well worth the effort; it totally lifts the whole dish. But remember that canned crab bisque is available – one or two tablespoons will be enough.

SERVES 4-6

5 cups Fish Stock (see p.221)
½-¾ cup (8-12 tablespoons) unsalted
    butter
1 tablespoon olive oil
2 onions, finely chopped
1-2 oz (25-50 g) bone marrow, chopped
    (optional)
1¼ cups arborio rice

8 oz (225 g) white crab meat, shredded
Salt and freshly ground white pepper
1-2 tablespoons finely grated Parmesan
    (optional)
Crab Bisque (see p.16) or canned
    (optional)
Parmesan flakes (optional)
Olive oil

Bring the fish or crab stock to the simmer. Melt ½ cup (8 tablespoons) of the butter with the olive oil, add the onions and cook for 3-4 minutes without coloring. As the onions begin to soften, add the bone marrow, if using. Add the rice and cook for 2-3 minutes. Now add two ladles of hot stock, keeping the rice over a medium heat. The hot stock will create a steam and immediately begin to evaporate. Because you only add a ladle at a time, the rice will absorb the stock without becoming totally encased. This is the process that helps cream the risotto. Continue to add the stock a little at a time until the rice is tender; this will take about 20 minutes. The finished texture of the rice should have the slightest bite.

Add the crab meat and the remaining butter and season with salt and pepper. I also like to add a little Parmesan to lift the taste. The consistency should not be at all stodgy but rich and creamy. Some crab bisque can be added to the finished risotto to improve the flavor and consistency even more; use a few spoonfuls.

The risotto is now ready to serve. If you are using crab bisque, spoon the risotto into bowls and pour some bisque around. The risotto can also be garnished with Parmesan flakes and a trickle of olive oil.

Variations

This recipe can be used for lobster, prawn or shrimp risotto. Mussels also make a good risotto. Cook them first in fish stock, then use the resulting mussel stock for the risotto. Don't add the cooked mussels to the rice until the end, otherwise they will be overcooked and tough.

Leek and Parmesan Risotto with a Warm Poached Egg

The traditional way to poach an egg is to bring a deep pan of water to a rolling boil. Add a generous amount of wine or malt vinegar, then crack the egg into the water. Poach for about 3 minutes until the white has set. Remove from the pan and place in a bowl of cold water to stop the cooking.

SERVES 4

5 cups Vegetable Stock (see p.223) or
    Chicken Stock (see p.222)
1 lb (450 g) leeks, trimmed and sliced
¾ cup (12 tablespoons) unsalted butter
2 onions, finely chopped
1 small garlic clove, crushed
1¼ cups arborio rice

3-4 tablespoons grated Parmesan
Salt and freshly ground white pepper
4 poached eggs
2-3 tablespoons Basic Vinaigrette (see
    p.241) or seasoned olive oil
1 tablespoon snipped fresh chives
Fresh Parmesan flakes (optional)

Bring the stock to the boil and add the sliced leeks. Bring back to the boil and drain the leeks off, reserving the leeks and stock separately. Melt the butter in a large pan, add the onions and garlic and cook for a few minutes without coloring until softened. Add the rice and cook for a further minute. Start to add the hot stock a ladle at a time and cook over a medium heat, allowing the rice to absorb almost all the stock before adding more stock. Continue to add, cook and stir until the rice is softening but not getting to a purée creamed stage; this will take about 20 minutes.

Stir in the Parmesan. The more you add, the richer the taste will become. The Parmesan will also thicken the risotto so add more stock to give a loose consistency if necessary. Add the leeks, season with salt and pepper and warm through. Spoon into the bowls and sit a warm poached egg on top. Mix the dressing or olive oil with the chives and spoon a little over the eggs. Sprinkle with some Parmesan flakes to finish.

Main Courses

In my television show you've seen me cook main courses from "ox cheeks" to "collar of bacon." I love showing you how to enjoy ingredients that aren't frequently used. But, remember: you can always adapt any of my recipes to the fish or meat you want to use. So, relax and have a go!

ABOVE *Roast Parsnip and Chestnut Crumble on Bubble and Squeak (see p.118).*
LEFT *Homemade Pork Pie (see p.92).*

I must admit if I'm cooking for myself and maybe a few friends I don't worry too much about balancing all the dishes; I tend just to cook what I feel like eating. However, balancing dishes is very important. Making sure that all the dishes aren't coated with cream sauces or too rich, for example, will give you a healthier and tastier meal.

The chapter has been broken down into smaller sections: Fish, Meat and Poultry, Vegetarian Dishes and Vegetables. Amongst these there are some more features of savory crumbles and tarts to keep you busy!

Fish

I've kept this part of the chapter relatively short, because the majority of dishes in the Starters section are fish, all of which are suitable to serve as main courses as well.

Cooking with fish is so enjoyable, the first advantage being the variety available, all with their different textures, colors and flavors. The texture of the fish will also determine how it should be cooked: pan-fried, deep-fried, broiled, braised or stewed.

One of my favorite fish is cod (you can probably tell, I've featured four cod dishes in this chapter!). A fresh, thick cod fillet is built up of large white flakes, and when simply broiled or pan-fried with just a tablespoon of butter and kept moist, the center of the flakes become almost transparent and juicy.

When I ask for fillets, I do mean fillets. Your fishmonger should be able to help you out with this. A lot of cod, for instance, is sold as steaks cut straight through the bone. It looks very nice but can be difficult to handle when eating. On top of that, cutting straight through will break down the texture of the fish, losing those lovely large flakes.

Skate is different altogether. This is normally sold on the bone and as skate wings. When cooking a skate wing dish, it's usually pan-fried and finished with butter, capers and parsley. Well, in one or two of these skate dishes I'm using fillets. These are quite easy to cut away from the bone and when pan-fried golden brown and crispy can become part of a whole dish a lot easier to eat. Sitting the fillet on top of salads or pasta works really well and you certainly can't do that if it's a straight skate wing!

All the fish dishes in this chapter can be adapted to the fish you want to use. So instead of cod or skate, why not try the recipe with monkfish, halibut, salmon or even something else?

Roast Cod on Potatoes with Fried Anchovies

This has to be my favorite fish dish in the book. Another cod dish? Well, as with most of the recipes, another fish can be used or you can leave the fish out and serve the dish as a warm potato salad with crispy anchovies. Marinated anchovies are sold loosely, not in cans.

Because I'm roasting this cod, I want to keep the skin on. When shallow-fried then roasted, cod skin comes up very crisp and tasty; it's good enough to eat on its own!

SERVES 4

1 lb (450 g) new potatoes
Salt and freshly ground white pepper
⅔ cup Vierge Dressing (see p.243) or olive oil
Juice of 1 lemon
2 tablespoons unsalted butter
2 teaspoons cooking oil
4 (6-8 oz) (175-225 g) cod fillets
12 marinated anchovies
1 teaspoon self-rising flour
¼ teaspoon cayenne

2-3 tablespoons milk
Oil for deep-frying
1 tablespoon fine or chopped capers
2 shallots or ½ onion, very finely chopped
½ teaspoon chopped fresh parsley
1 teaspoon chopped fresh cilantro
1 teaspoon chopped fresh tarragon
1 teaspoon chopped fresh basil
A few green salad leaves (optional)

Pre-heat the oven to 400°F (200°C).

Cook the new potatoes, then peel off the skin. Cut into ¼ inch (5mm) slices while still warm, then season with salt and pepper. Add 1-2 tablespoons of dressing or olive oil and the juice of ½ lemon. Season with salt and pepper and keep warm.

Melt the butter and oil in a hot pan. Season the cod with salt and pepper and place in the pan skin-side-down. Cook until deep in color, then turn over and finish cooking in the oven for 5-8 minutes, depending on the thickness of the cod.

Split the anchovies through the center. Mix the flour with the cayenne and a pinch of salt. Dip the anchovies in the milk, then roll in the cayenne flour. Deep-fry in hot oil until very crispy. If you don't have a deep-fat fryer, cook them in about ¼ inch (5 mm) of hot oil in a frying pan, but don't let it get so hot that it smokes, and keep turning the fish in the pan until they are crispy.

To finish the dish, warm the remaining dressing or oil and add the capers and shallots or onion with a squeeze of lemon juice and the herbs. Season with salt and pepper. The dressing should be served warm.

Spoon some potatoes onto plates and top with a few green salad leaves. Spoon the dressing all around and sit a few fried anchovy fillets on top of the dressing. Finish the dish with the roasted cod fillet on top with the crispy skin-side showing. Brush with a little butter to finish.

Fried Anchovies

Pan-fried Cod on Fennel and Potato Salad with Tartar Dressing

Cod, chips (French fries) and tartar sauce is probably Britain's most famous and classic fish dish, and cooked well with a good, crispy batter and a tartar made with fresh mayonnaise, you can't beat it (see overleaf). I decided to use nearly all of those tastes in this dish: the fresh cod, potatoes and tartar sauce flavor without the mayonnaise. To this I've added some fresh fennel which, with its slight anise flavor, really helps the potatoes and fish. You can, of course, leave out the fennel and I promise you'll still enjoy this lighter version of our old favorite.

SERVES 4

4 (6-8 oz) (175-225 g) cod fillets
2 tablespoons all-purpose flour

4 tablespoons unsalted butter
1 tablespoon olive oil

For the Dressing

2 teaspoons capers
2 teaspoons chopped cocktail gherkins
   or dill pickles
2 teaspoons chopped shallot or onion

½ bunch of fresh parsley
1-2 tablespoons olive oil
Salt and freshly ground black pepper

For the Fennel and Potatoes

2 large fennel bulbs
2 lemons
10 oz (275 g) new potatoes

¼ cup Basic Vinaigrette
   (see p.241)

To make the dressing, place the capers, gherkins or pickles and shallot or onion in a food processor and process until almost puréed. Add the parsley and 1 tablespoon of olive oil. Continue to process until the parsley is finely chopped. Season with salt and pepper. If the dressing is very thick, simply add more olive oil. This dressing keeps well for 24 hours in the refrigerator.

To cook the fennel, top and tail the bulbs and remove some of the core at the base. Bring about 5 cups of water to the boil (enough to cover the fennel) with the juice of 1 lemon and a pinch of salt. Place the fennel into the water and cover with a lid, bring back to the boil, then simmer until just tender; this will take 15-20 minutes. Leave to cool. Cut the fennel in half lengthwise, then each half into 5-6 slices lengthwise.

Meanwhile, boil the new potatoes until tender, then drain, peel off the skins and cut the potatoes in half. Mix the basic dressing with the juice of the remaining lemon and add to the new potatoes and fennel slices. Season with salt and pepper and bring up to the simmer.

To cook the cod, lightly flour and season each fillet and brush with butter on the skin side. Heat a frying pan with a little olive oil. Lay the cod butter-side-down into the pan and cook until golden brown. Turn the fish in the pan and continue to cook. The cod will take about 6-8 minutes to cook.

To serve, spoon the tartar dressing into bowls or plates and sit the fennel and potatoes on top. Finish by sitting the cod on to the garnish.

OVERLEAF *Clockwise, starting at the front:*
Deep-fried Cod in Batter (see p.72);
Pan-fried Cod on Pecorino Mashed Potatoes and Spinach (see p.73);
extra Fried Anchovies (see p.66);
Pan-fried Cod on Fennel and Potato Salad with Tartar Dressing (see p.68);
Roast Cod on Potatoes with Fried Anchovies (see p.66).

Deep-fried Cod in Batter

This must be the quickest batter to make. It's just lager-style beer and some salt and self-rising flour. The only secret is to make sure the batter is very thick, almost too thick. As the cod is cooking, the batter will soufflé, keeping it light and crisp (see preceding pages). If the batter is too thin, it tends to stick to the fish and become heavy. You can use the same recipe for any deep-fried fish, sausages or whatever. It also eats well with Tomato Sauce (see p.233).

SERVES 4

3½ cups self-rising flour
Salt and freshly ground black pepper
4 (6-8 oz) (175-225 g) cod fillets,
   skinned and boned

2½ cups lager-style beer
A pinch of salt
Oil for deep-frying

For the Tartar Sauce

1¼ cups Mayonnaise (see p.242)
2 tablespoons gherkins or dill pickles,
   chopped
2 tablespoons capers, chopped

2 tablespoons onion, finely chopped
2 teaspoons chopped fresh parsley
A squeeze of lemon juice

Season a spoonful of flour with salt and pepper. Lightly dust each fillet in the flour.

Whisk half the remaining flour into the lager-style beer with a pinch of salt, then gradually add the flour a spoonful at a time to make a thick batter. Dip the cod into the batter. Heat the oil to 350°F (180°C), then fry the cod until golden.

To make the sauce, mix all the ingredients together and season with lemon juice, salt and pepper. Serve with the crispy fried cod.

Pan-fried Cod on Pecorino Mashed Potatoes and Spinach

You don't have to stick to cod with this recipe: any firm, white-fleshed fish can be used and taste just as good (see pp. 70–71).

Pecorino is an Italian ewes' milk cheese with a similar texture to Parmesan. I like to use smoked Pecorino for extra taste. Pecorino cheeses were introduced to me by Giovanni, an Italian friend who lives in South Wales. Giovanni makes his own "Pecorinos" with Welsh ewes' milk – and it works! The cheese is lovely. If you have trouble finding Pecorino, just use Parmesan.

All I do with this recipe is add grated smoked Pecorino to hot mashed potatoes to give you a delicious cheesy mash. Of course, you can use the cheesy mash with any recipe that calls for mashed potatoes.

SERVES 4

1 tablespoon all-purpose flour
Salt and freshly ground white pepper
4 (6-8 oz) (175-225 g) cod fillets, skinned
1 tablespoon cooking oil
8 tablespoons (½ cup) unsalted butter

3-4 tablespoons Fish Stock (see p.221) or water
2 lb (900 g) spinach, picked and washed
Juice of ½ lemon
2 cups or ½ recipe Mashed Potatoes (see p.133)
1-1½ cups grated Romano cheese

Lightly flour and season the cod with salt and pepper. Heat a frying pan with the oil and 2 tablespoons of the butter. When the pan is hot and the butter bubbling, add the cod and cook for about 3-4 minutes on each side, keeping the pan hot, until the fish is golden brown. Always cook the presentation or skin-side-down first. When the fish colors, it will show every line of the fillet and also hold the fish together a lot better.

While the fish is cooking, bring the stock or water to the boil with 2 tablespoons of butter. Add the spinach leaves and stir for 2-3 minutes. The spinach will cook quickly and create a spinach liquid in the pan. Season with salt and pepper, drain off the spinach and re-boil the liquid. Whisk in the remaining butter to make a spinach butter sauce. Taste and adjust the seasoning if necessary and add the lemon juice to lift the flavor.

Warm the mashed potatoes with 1 cup of cheese. Taste and add the remaining cheese, or more if you wish.

Spoon the potatoes onto plates and sit some spinach on top. Arrange the fish on top. You now have a tower of flavors. Pour the spinach butter sauce around and serve.

Fillet of Skate with Red Peppers, Potatoes, Capers and Bayonne Ham

Filleting skate is quite unusual – skate wings are normally cooked on the bone – but it really suits this dish. It's a simple recipe with not too many flavors, just enough to help each other. Bayonne is a cured ham usually made in Orthez near Béarn in southwest France. It has a similar texture to Parma ham but the flavors are different. Bayonne is usually lightly smoked to lift the taste. If you can't find any, substitute Parma ham. Cut the thin slices into ½ inch (1 cm) strips ready to fry until crisp. This recipe also works well with halibut cheeks or monkfish instead of skate.

SERVES 4

2 red bell peppers	4 (6 oz) (175 g) skate fillets
Juice of 1 lemon	1 tablespoon all-purpose flour
6 tablespoons olive oil	2 tablespoons unsalted butter
Salt and freshly ground white pepper	4-6 slices Bayonne ham, cut into pieces
8-12 oz (225-350 g) new potatoes, peeled, cooked and sliced	Mixed salad leaves
2 teaspoons small capers	2 tablespoons Basic Vinaigrette (see p.241)

Core and halve the peppers lengthwise, remove the seeds and cut into ½ inch (1 cm) slices lengthwise. Mix the lemon juice with 4 tablespoons of olive oil and season with salt and pepper and pour over the potatoes. Fry the peppers in a little olive oil, coloring and softening slightly, then mix with the potatoes and capers.

Dust the skate with flour, brush with butter and season with salt and pepper. Pre-heat a frying pan and brush with olive oil. Sit the wings in the pan, presentation-side-down, and fry quickly for 2 minutes, then turn and cook for a further minute.

Meanwhile, heat another pan and fry the ham in virtually no fat, cooking and tossing until crisp.

Divide the potatoes and peppers between the plates. Toss the salad leaves in a little dressing and arrange on top. Sit the skate on the leaves and spoon the crisp ham over the top.

Note

Salad leaves are not essential for any of the fish dishes, but they always help the texture.

Fillet of Skate with Red Peppers, Potatoes,
Capers and Bayonne Ham.

Pan-fried Skate with Ratatouille Salad

The skate in this dish is also filleted and shallow-fried. If you can't find skate fillets, monk fish or halibut cheeks would also work well.

SERVES 4

2 red bell peppers	1 tablespoon all-purpose flour
1 green bell pepper	4 (6 oz) (175 g) skate fillets
2 small zucchini	1 cup Basic Vinaigrette (see p.241)
1 large onion, thickly sliced	6 fresh basil leaves (optional)
2 tablespoons olive oil	1-2 teaspoons Pesto Sauce (see p.235)
4 tablespoons unsalted butter	(optional)
4 cups sliced mushrooms	Green salad leaves
Salt and freshly ground white pepper	1 eggplant, sliced and fried (see p.42)

Core and halve the peppers lengthwise, remove the seeds and cut into ½ inch (1 cm) slices lengthwise. Slice the zucchini at an angle to give oval slices. Fry the onion and peppers in a heavy-based pan in a little olive oil and butter until softened. Add the zucchini and cook for 1 minute, then remove from the heat. Cook the mushrooms separately in a very hot pan in a little olive oil, then add to the other vegetables. Season with salt and pepper.

Lightly flour the skate fillets and brush with butter. Heat a frying pan and brush with oil. Sit the fillets buttered-side-down in the pan and fry quickly for 2 minutes on one side, then 1 minute on the other until golden brown.

Mix the vinaigrette with the basil leaves or pesto, if using, and use a little to dress the salad leaves. Add the ratatouille to the dressing and spoon onto plates. Sit the leaves on top and finish with the fish and eggplant.

Variations

Another skate dish that I enjoy is one that is cooked on the bone. The skate is shallow-fried in olive oil and butter for 3-4 minutes on each side until the flesh is crisp and golden brown. Arrange the skate on a plate and surround with some Lemon Butter Sauce (see p.228), finishing with some crunchy brown shrimp and parsley in nut brown butter.

The best shrimp to use are the small, brown variety. To pick them, simply pull off the heads and small tails and leave the rest of the shell on the tail itself. The shell is crispy without being too hard. To make the butter nut brown, heat a frying pan and add some butter. It should be bubbling and beginning to color almost immediately. When it's just turning brown but not burnt, add the shrimp tails, a squeeze of lemon juice and season with salt and pepper. Finish with chopped fresh parsley and spoon over the skate.

Sea Bass on Minestrone

This sauce is almost like a minestrone soup, with the flavor of all the vegetables cooked in a tomato coulis. The dish eats well with noodles or with the fish on mashed potatoes. Sea bass is not the only fish that can be used. Most white fish will also eat well. A seafood minestrone of scallops, prawns, mussels and cockles (small clams) is a real winner.

SERVES 4

4 tablespoons unsalted butter
1 tablespoon olive oil
2 carrots, diced
1 large onion, diced
2 celery stalks, diced
1 garlic clove, crushed
1 medium zucchini, diced
½ leek, diced
1½ cups white wine

⅔ cup Fish Stock (see p.221)
⅔ cup Tomato Coulis (see p.232)
4 (6–8 oz) (175–225 g) sea bass fillets
2 tomatoes, skinned and diced
8–10 fresh basil leaves, cut into squares
12–15 fresh tarragon leaves, cut into squares
1–2 teaspoons Pesto Sauce (see p.235) (optional)

Melt half the butter with the olive oil, then add the carrots, onion, celery and garlic. Cook without coloring for a few minutes. Cook the zucchini and leek separately in a tablespoon of butter so that they retain their green color. Once cooked, allow them to cool, then add them toward the end of cooking. Once the vegetables have softened, add the white wine and boil to reduce until almost dry. Add the stock and boil to reduce by half. Add the tomato coulis and simmer for 10–12 minutes until the sauce has a broth consistency.

Arrange the fish on a buttered and seasoned baking sheet and cook under a hot broiler for 5–10 minutes, leaving the skin golden and crispy.

While the fish is cooking, add the tomatoes, herbs, zucchini and leeks to the minestrone, bring to the simmer and add the remaining butter. Finish with the pesto sauce, if liked. Spoon the minestrone sauce into some bowls and sit the fish on top.

Variations

To make this into a more complete meal, cook some noodles and toss in butter. Sit the noodles in the center of the bowls and spoon the sauce around. Arrange the fish on top.

Try serving the dish with mashed potatoes, leaving out the pesto sauce, and spooning some of the sauce onto the mash before sitting the fish on top and spooning the remaining sauce around.

Stuffed Herrings

This dish eats well on its own simply with a squeeze of lemon or served with a Mustard Cream Sauce (see p.79).

SERVES 4

8 (4–5 oz) herring fillets

For the Stuffing

4 medium slices white bread, crumbed
3 tablespoons butter
1 large onion, finely chopped
2 slices smoked bacon,
    finely diced
½ teaspoon chopped fresh sage

¼ teaspoon chopped fresh thyme
½ teaspoon chopped fresh parsley
1 oz (25 g) bone marrow, finely diced
    (optional)
Salt and freshly ground black pepper

Pre-heat the oven to 400°F (200°C).

To make the stuffing, remove the crusts from the sliced bread and crumb the slices. Melt 1 tablespoon of the butter, add the chopped onion and cook without coloring for 2–3 minutes. Add the bacon and herbs and continue to cook for 2 minutes. Allow to cool. Mix with the breadcrumbs, diced bone marrow, if using, and the remaining butter. Season with salt and pepper. The texture of this stuffing should just hold and bind together if squeezed in your hand.

The herrings should be filleted and as many fine bones removed as possible. Lay out four fillets and divide and spread the stuffing over them. Cover with the other fillets. Before cooking, wrap the fish in a layer of buttered foil. Bake them in the oven for 12–15 minutes.

Herrings with Green Onion and Bacon Potato Cakes

These herring fillets are broiled and arranged on top of potato cakes. They can then be served with a wedge of lemon or with a mustard cream sauce.

SERVES 4

8 (4–5 oz) (115-150g) herring fillets
Olive oil or unsalted butter

4 Green Onion Potato Cakes with bacon
  (see p.133)

For the Mustard Cream Sauce

4 tablespoons unsalted butter
1 shallot, chopped
1 carrot, chopped
1 celery stalk, chopped
1 slice bacon, chopped

A few tarragon leaves
1½ cups white wine
1¼ cups Fish Stock (see p.221)
¼–⅓ cup heavy whipping cream
1-3 teaspoons stone-ground mustard

Melt 1 tablespoon of butter and cook the vegetables, bacon and tarragon without coloring until they soften. Add the white wine and boil to reduce until almost dry. Add the stock and boil to reduce by half. Add the cream and cook for 8-10 minutes. Strain the sauce and whisk in the remaining butter. Add the mustard a little at a time until you have the right strength.

Meanwhile, brush the herring fillets with a little oil or butter and cook under a hot broiler for 5-10 minutes.

Sit the potato cakes in the center of the plates, spoon the sauce around and lay two herring fillets on top of each potato cake.

Variations

The potato cake works well using spinach instead of bacon and green onions (see p.133). Cook 1 lb (450 g) of washed spinach in 2 tablespoons of butter for a few minutes until tender, then drain, cool and chop. Add the spinach to the potato mix and proceed as for that recipe. They eat particularly well with fish dishes.

Cooked mushrooms, bacon, onion and many other ingredients can also be added to the potato cakes.

Fish on Spinach with a Cider and Mussel Sauce

I've just called this "fish" because so many fish work well with this recipe: cod, halibut, sea bass, monkfish – the list could go on. Make sure whichever fish you choose, it is well filleted with all bones removed. White fish should be skinned as well.

SERVES 4

4 (6-8 oz) (175-225 g) fish fillets	6 tablespoons unsalted butter
2 tablespoons all-purpose flour	2 lb (900 g) fresh spinach, washed

For the Mussel Cooking Liquid

1 tablespoon unsalted butter	1 star anise (optional)
1 onion, roughly chopped	1½ cups dry white wine
1 carrot, roughly chopped	2½ cups Fish Stock (see p.221) or water
2 celery stalks, roughly chopped	2 lb (900 g) fresh mussels, scrubbed and
½ leek, roughly chopped	bearded
1 bay leaf (optional)	
1 sprig of fresh thyme	

For the Cider Sauce

12 oz (350 g) shallots or onions, sliced	1-2 bottles dry hard cider
into rings	⅓-½ cup heavy whipping cream
2 tablespoons unsalted butter	Salt and freshly ground white pepper
A pinch of saffron (optional)	

To cook the mussels, melt the butter and fry the vegetables, bay leaf, thyme and star anise, if using, for 8-10 minutes without coloring. Add the wine and boil to reduce until almost dry. Add the stock or water, bring to the boil and cook for a few minutes. Add the mussels and bring to the boil, stirring. Once the stock is boiling, the mussels will be opening and cooking. Drain and reserve the cooking liquid. Discard any mussels that have not opened and pick the rest from their shells. Keep them in a few spoonfuls of cooking liquid to keep them moist.

To make the cider sauce, soften the shallots in a tablespoon of butter with the saffron, if using. Add the cider and boil to reduce by three-quarters. Add the mussel stock and continue to reduce by half. Add half the cream, bring to a simmer and simmer for a few minutes. Check for taste and consistency and season with salt and pepper. If the sauce is too thin, reduce a little more. Add a tablespoon or two of butter to enrich the flavor.

The fish should be seasoned and lightly dusted in flour before being pan-fried, or just seasoned if being broiled. Cod will take 3-4 minutes on each side.

While the fish is cooking, melt the butter in a large pan and add the spinach. Cook and stir for 2-3 minutes until tender. Add the mussels to the fish sauce and warm through. Spoon the spinach onto plates and sit the fish on top. Spoon the sauce over the fish, forming a small pile of shallots on top of each fillet.

Poultry and Meat

In this section, I've tried to choose cuts of meat that I feel aren't used often enough, in restaurants or at home. These cuts have a lot more flavor and texture than many of the fine cuts such as fillet of beef. Given a slow cooking process, the wonderful textures are developed to the full. Braised ox cheeks are sensational, so is breast of lamb and haunch of venison. Pork belly is another winner. Left in a spicy marinade for 24 hours, then roasted and glazed with honey, it is transformed into something quite magical. I've also included roasted knuckles and explain how to make good pork scratchings. These again are cuts that we don't seem to use. How often do you make your own pork scratchings? Perhaps it's time you had a go.

Another dish I have included is Homemade Corned Beef. I always used to wonder how corned beef was made and how it got its texture. (I'm still not quite sure how they manage to keep that deep red color!) Well, after reading through several cookbooks and plenty of trials I eventually finished with the recipe in this chapter. It is so simple and easy to make. Pork Pie is another homey favorite.

You'll also find a few duck dishes and, of course, chicken dishes, one of them with a Scottish theme served sitting on braised pearl barley, which normally features in Scotch broth.

So if you're "scratching" for an idea to fill your "belly" just "knuckle" down and read this chapter!

TOP *Grilled Chicken Breast with Braised Pearl Barley,*
Lemon and Thyme (see p.84).
BOTTOM *Grilled Chicken on Red Wine*
Onions and Mushrooms (see p.85).

Grilled Chicken Breast with Braised Pearl Barley, Lemon and Thyme

This really is a simple dish, not too many ingredients but packed with textures and tastes (see preceding page). Instead of simmering the barley on the stove, it cooks evenly if you put it in a pre-heated oven at 350°F (180°C).

SERVES 4

1 large onion, finely chopped
¾–1 cup (12–16 tablespoons) unsalted
    butter, softened but not melted
3¾ cups Chicken Stock (see p.222)
1 leek, sliced or diced

½ cup pearl barley
1 teaspoon chopped fresh thyme
Juice of 1–2 lemons
4 chicken breasts
Salt and freshly ground black pepper

To braise the barley, cook the chopped onion in 4 tablespoons of the butter, without coloring, until softened. Bring 2½ cups of the chicken stock to the boil, add the leeks and cook for 30 seconds. Strain, reserving both stock and leeks. Add the pearl barley to the onions and cook for another 1–2 minutes. Add the stock and bring to the simmer. Cover with a lid and cook over a low heat, stirring continuously, until the barley becomes tender; this will take 30–40 minutes. Add more stock if the barley becomes dry. The remaining 1¼ cups of chicken stock can be boiled until reduced by half to leave you with a good, strong stock.

Mix 8–10 tablespoons of the butter with the thyme and lemon juice. (This can be made at any time and will keep in the refrigerator for as long as the butter will last.)

The chicken breasts eat very well if cooked on a hot ridged grill pan or open barbecue. They can also be pan-fried or cooked under the broiler. They will take about 15 minutes.

To finish the barley, add a tablespoon of butter and the leeks and warm through. If there is still a lot of excess chicken stock, simply pour it off. Re-boil the reduced chicken stock, then gradually add and whisk in enough of the lemon and thyme butter until you have a smooth sauce consistency. Season with salt and pepper. Spoon the barley onto the center of a warmed serving plate and pour the sauce around. Slice the chicken breast through the middle and place on top of the barley.

Grilled Chicken on Red Wine Onions and Mushrooms

This dish is very rich; the flavor of the red onions cooked in red wine eats beautifully (see p.83). I recommend Portobello mushrooms; they have a good flavor and texture. This mushroom and red wine garnish also works well with lamb and beef.

SERVES 4

4 tablespoons unsalted butter
8-10 large red onions, sliced
⅓ cup demerara or light brown sugar
1¼ cups red wine vinegar
Salt and freshly ground black pepper
3 cups red wine

2 tablespoons crème de cassis (optional)
8 Portobello or 12 large white
    mushrooms
4 chicken breasts
1¼ cups Red Wine Sauce (see p.230)

Pre-heat the oven to 400°F (200°C).

Melt half the butter in a large pan, add the onions and cook for a few minutes without coloring until they begin to soften. Add the sugar and red wine vinegar and boil to reduce until almost dry. Season with salt and pepper. Add the wine and reduce until almost dry. Season again with salt and pepper and stir in the crème de cassis, if using.

Remove the stalks from the mushrooms and tear off the outer skin from the mushrooms. This is not essential but makes them even more tender. Lay them upside down on a buttered and seasoned baking sheet, brush with butter and season again. Cook under the broiler for 4-6 minutes until tender.

Meanwhile, cook the chicken on an open gas grill or barbecue or on a hot ridged grill pan, or just fry in a little butter until golden, then finish in the pre-heated oven at for 8-10 minutes. Warm the red wine sauce.

To serve the dish, divide the onions between four bowls (there may well be enough for more!), then sit the mushrooms on top. Carve the chicken through the center and arrange on top of the mushrooms. Pour the warm sauce around.

Variations

For a lighter sauce, take any of the red onion trimmings after slicing them and cook in a tablespoon of butter for a few minutes until softened. Add 2½ cups of red wine and reduce until almost dry. Add 2 cups of chicken stock and reduce by half. Strain through a sieve and whisk in 4-6 tablespoons of unsalted butter. This will give you a lighter red wine sauce that can be puréed in a food processor or blender to make it even lighter!

Crispy Roast Duck Breasts with Parsnip Purée

The duck breasts I use for this recipe are called magrets. *This is a duck breast that has been completely removed from the bone and has no wing attached. This breast can then have the skin removed or left on. I prefer to leave the skin on, as this gives a crispy finish.* Magret *duck breasts usually come vacuum-packed from France and are ready to cook. If you can't get* magrets, *simply roast duck breasts still on the carcass, then remove them from the bone once cooked and rested.*

Serves 4

4 *magret* duck breasts	1 lb (450 g) parsnips
1 tablespoon vegetable or olive oil	5 tablespoons unsalted butter
Salt and freshly ground black pepper	1 recipe Cranberry Gravy (see p.238)
4 teaspoons clear honey	

Pre-heat the oven to 400°F (200°C).

First score the fat on the duck breasts with a sharp knife all the way across (right to left) about 1/16 inch (2 mm) apart. The fat only needs to be scored and not cut through into the flesh. Pre-heat a roasting pan on top of the stove with the oil. Season the scored duck breasts with salt and pepper. Sit the breasts skin-side-down into the pan. This will create some spitting from the pan as all water content from the fat will cook out. Once the breasts are cooking fast, turn the heat down to medium and continue to cook the breasts fat-side-down until dark and almost burnt. The layer of skin will have cooked right down almost like a confit. Turn the breasts over and finish in the pre-heated oven for 6-10 minutes until the flesh is cooked to medium, depending on the thickness of the breast; a large, thick breast will take 8-10 minutes. Once cooked, the skin will be dark, rich and crispy, almost like duck crackling!

This can now be made even tastier if honey is spooned on top and glazed under the broiler. Before serving the breasts, it's best to leave them to rest for 5-10 minutes as this will allow the meat to become more tender.

To make the parsnip purée, peel and split the parsnips lengthwise into quarters, and cut out the woody centers. Boil in salted water for about 15 minutes until tender, drain and shake dry. Add the salt and pepper and butter and mash the parsnips. Push through a sieve to get a smooth-textured purée.

The *magrets* can be left whole or sliced diagonally and arranged on a plate. Serve the parsnip purée separately or shape it between two large spoons to give an oval shape and serve on the plate with the duck. Pour some of the cranberry gravy onto the dish and serve.

Crispy Roast Duck Breasts with Parsnip Purée

Confit of Duck

This is a classic French dish that can also work with goose or pork. In my last book, the duck legs were steeped in a marinade for a few days. Well, this recipe is without the marinade and these duck legs will just be salted for 24 hours before cooking.

SERVES 4

4 duck legs   2 lb (900 g) lard or goose fat, melted
2 teaspoons rock sea salt

Trim the legs of any remaining feather stalks and remove the knuckle on the underside of the thigh. The skin can also be scored around the top of the drumstick knuckle so this will shrink while cooking and reveal the bone. Salt the legs on the skin side and chill for 24 hours. This will draw any water from the fat and ensure that the skin is crisp when the legs are cooked.

Pre-heat the oven to 325°F (160°C).

Sit the legs in a casserole dish and cover with melted lard. Bring just to a light simmer, cover with a lid and cook in the oven for 1½-2 hours. To check the legs, remove one from the fat and push the skin side. When you feel the meat is starting to become tender and give, remove from the heat and leave to cool in the fat.

Transfer the legs to a clean dish and cover completely in fat. They will keep chilled almost indefinitely.

To roast the legs, pre-heat the oven to 400°F (200°C). Remove the legs from the fat and cut off the end knuckle. Cook in the pre-heated oven for 15-20 minutes until crispy.

Confit of Duck with Orange Sauce and Buttered Spinach

This is a variation on the original confit (see p.88). When salting the duck legs, add the zest of one orange and leave it with the legs during the cooking stage. This will help infuse the orange taste. To add even more orange taste to the duck, finely grate the zest of an orange, add it to some clear honey and use to glaze the roasted duck confit and give a sharp orange flavor.

SERVES 4

4 Confit of Duck legs (see p.88).

For the Orange Sauce

1¼ cups Red Wine Sauce (see p.230)

Zest of 1 orange
Juice of 1 orange

For the Buttered Spinach

2 lb (900 g) spinach, washed
4 tablespoons unsalted butter

Salt and freshly ground black pepper

To make an orange sauce, start with a red wine sauce. During the cooking of the vegetables, add the orange zest and follow the recipe until the red wine has reduced in volume. Add the orange juice and boil until reduced by three-quarters. Continue with the recipe, adding the veal *jus* or alternative, and cook for 20-30 minutes, pushing the finished sauce through a sieve. The orange sauce is now ready and has a richness helped by the red wine.

To cook the spinach, make sure all excess water has been shaken off the leaves. Melt the butter in a hot pan. Once the butter begins to bubble, add the spinach and stir with a wooden spoon, keeping the pan at a high temperature. The spinach will cook very quickly. After 2-3 minutes, season the spinach with salt and pepper. Drain off any excess liquid and the spinach is ready.

To serve spinach with the duck, it's nice to divide the spinach between individual plates or bowls and sit each glazed duck leg confit on top. Just finish by pouring the orange sauce around.

Peppered Confit of Duck with Peppercorn Sauce

Cook the duck legs as for the basic salted recipe (see p.88). Once cooked and removed from the fat, sprinkle finely crushed black peppercorns on top of each leg. The legs can now be roasted and glazed.

SERVES 4

4 Confit of Duck legs (see p.88).

For the Peppercorn Sauce

2 teaspoons green peppercorns, lightly
   crushed
2 shallots, finely chopped
2 tablespoons unsalted butter
¼ cup brandy

¾ cup dry white wine
1¼ cups Veal *Jus* (see p.224) or
   alternative (see p.226)
⅔ cup heavy whipping cream

To make a peppercorn sauce, cook the peppercorns and shallots in the butter until just softened. Add the brandy and boil to reduce until almost dry. Add the white wine and boil to reduce until almost dry. Add the veal *jus* or alternative, bring the sauce to the simmer and cook gently for 20 minutes. Add the heavy whipping cream (it will not curdle) and continue to cook and simmer for a few minutes. You should now have a good sauce consistency with a *café au lait* (milky coffee) color.

Boiled Collar of Bacon on Mustard Mashed Potatoes with Chive Liquid

I enjoy boiled bacon dishes. The beauty of boiling meat is that it creates its own stock as it cooks, which then becomes the base for the sauce.

Mashed potatoes go well with this dish. I normally don't even tamper with mashed potatoes, but mustard and bacon are good friends and using them to flavor the potatoes gives them a real bite. You can choose whatever mustard you prefer, but I recommend stone-ground, Dijon or English. My favorite is Dijon mash; not too hot but packed with flavor.

The combination of mustard mashed potatoes and bacon works so well. The potatoes eat equally well with almost any form of pork – roast leg or loin, sausages, or braised belly are just a few.

SERVES 4-6

2-3 lb (900 g-1.5 kg) smoked bacon collar or pork shoulder, rolled and rind removed
1 onion, roughly chopped
2 carrots, roughly chopped
2 celery stalks, roughly chopped
½ leek, roughly chopped
1 bay leaf

5-7½ cups Chicken Stock (see p.222) or water
½ cup (8 tablespoons) unsalted butter
Salt and freshly ground white pepper
3-4 cups or ¾ recipe Mashed Potatoes (see p.133)
About 1 tablespoon Dijon mustard

Soak the bacon in water for 24 hours before cooking to reduce the salt content.

Sit the bacon in a pan with the vegetables and bay leaf. Cover with the stock or water. Bring to the simmer and continue to simmer for 1-1½ hours. Leave to rest in the liquid for 20–30 minutes.

Drain off 2½ cups of the stock, bring to the boil and boil until reduced by half. Whisk in a spoonful of butter at a time to make a creamy sauce; you may find that 6 tablespoons is enough. You can use a hand blender to give a creamier consistency. Season with salt and pepper.

Add some mustard to the mashed potatoes a teaspoon at a time, tasting as you go until you have the mustard flavor you want. Spoon the potatoes onto plates. Add the chives to the liquid and spoon round the mash. Carve the bacon, two slices per portion, and arrange on top of the potatoes.

Homemade Pork Pie

A lot of dishes, like this one and the corned beef, sound hard work and you may think there is no point going to all that trouble. In fact, both recipes are very simple, and there's a great feeling of satisfaction when eating the homemade versions. They will never have the artificial pink color that most bought varieties have. Your pork pie will have a natural color with just a tinge of pink when finished (see p.62).

The meat I use for this recipe is belly pork, bought already skinned and boned. If you're buying from a butcher then try and get the pork coarsely ground. The pork pie filling must be made before the pastry as hot water crust must be molded while still warm. The pork pie can be made as a raised pie or tart-style pie. The pan I am using is 7 inches (18 cm) diameter by 3 inches (7.5 cm) deep. A springform pan would work for this. If you don't have a deep pie pan or dish use a 10 inch (25 cm) tart pan and follow the same method, but cook for about 1–1½ hours.

To finish the pie, it's best to fill the pan with a jelly made by using a good Chicken Stock (see p.222) boiled to reduce from 6 cups to 3¾ cups. Alternatively you can use a pork stock by cooking three or four pig's trotters in water for a few hours. This will create its own jelly that can be helped, if needed, with the addition of 1 tablespoon of gelatin per 2½ cups of stock.

Serves 8

2 tablespoons unsalted butter
2 onions, finely chopped
1 teaspoon chopped fresh sage
1 teaspoon chopped fresh thyme
1 level teaspoon ground mace
½ teaspoon English mustard powder

½ teaspoon allspice
2 lb (900 g) pork belly, coarsely ground
   or chopped
Salt and freshly ground white pepper
1 egg, beaten
3¾ –5 cups jellied stock

For the Pastry

2½ cups water
8 tablespoons lard

3½ cups all-purpose flour

Melt the butter in a pan. Once the butter begins to bubble, add the chopped onions and cook for a few minutes, without coloring, until just softened. While the onions are still warm, add the sage, thyme, mace, mustard and allspice. Allow to cool. Mix the onions and spices with the ground pork, making sure the meat is not over-beaten as this will break down the fat content and texture. Season generously with salt and pepper. It's important to make sure the mix is highly seasoned at the raw stage, as serving it cold will reduce the strength of the seasoning. Leave the filling in the refrigerator.

Pre-heat the oven to 425°F (220°C). Grease a pie pan and place it on a baking sheet.

Bring the water and lard to the boil. Sift the flour with a generous pinch of salt into a bowl, leaving a well in the center. Pour in the boiling water and lard and stir in the flour to form a dough. Knead lightly by hand (the pastry will be very warm) to give a smooth dough. Keep a quarter of the pastry warm to one side, then work the rest of the pastry on a lightly floured table by hand or with a rolling pin until just under ¼ inch (5 mm) thick. Sit the pastry in the pan and work by hand, starting from the center and gently pushing out to make the pastry thinner and to fill the pan. The finished pastry should be about ⅛ inch (3 mm) thick and ¼ inch (5 mm) above the top of the pan.

Fill the crust with the pork filling, packing it in just above the top of the pan. Fold the pastry around the top on to the mix and brush with the beaten egg. Roll out the remaining pastry to the same thickness and sit on top of the pie, pressing the edges together and cutting off any excess. Using a small cylinder pastry cutter or piping nozzle, cut a hole in the center and leave the cutter or nozzle sitting in the hole. The border of the pie can be pinched or pushed with a fork to give a simple patterned edge. Brush the pie with beaten egg.

Bake the pie immediately in the hot oven for 20 minutes, then reduce the oven temperature to 375°F (190°C) and cook for a further 1½-2 hours (30 minutes less if you are using a shallow pan). During the first 20 minutes the pie may color very quickly. Once it's reached golden stage cover lightly with aluminum foil, only covering the top and not the sides as this will slow down the cooking time.

Test whether the pie is ready either by feeling the filling through the hole in the center – the mix should be firm to the touch – or inserting a knife into the filling. It should feel tender and the knife will still be clean. Remove the pie from the oven and leave to cool for 30 minutes.

During cooking, the pork filling will have shrunk a little, leaving a border to be filled with jelly. Using a funnel or jug, pour 1¼ cups of the jellied stock into the pie. It will be absorbed by the meat, giving it a moister finish. Leave the pie to finish cooling, by which time the stock will be almost at jelly stage. Pour in the remaining stock until filled and jellied. It's now best to keep the pie in the refrigerator. See, it was worth it!

Boiled Collar of Bacon with Homemade Sauerkraut

Sauerkraut is a warm pickled cabbage. I used to eat sauerkraut a lot when I lived in Amsterdam in the late 70s and also when visiting my brother who lived in Germany. We would always have grilled bratwurst sausage with sauerkraut in a roll. I think these were the German answer to hot dogs and ketchup!

Sauerkraut is often cooked with bacon to help the flavor. I decided to keep the sauerkraut "vegetarian." Serve it with the boiled bacon and mustard seed sauce.

SERVES 4-6

1 (2-3 lb) (900 g-1.5 kg) bacon collar or pork shoulder boned, skinned, rolled and tied
1 onion, roughly chopped
2 carrots, roughly chopped
2 celery stalks, roughly chopped
1 bay leaf

Chicken Stock (see p.222) or water to cover bacon
⅔ cup heavy whipping cream
2 tablespoons butter
1-2 teaspoons mustard seed
Salt and freshly ground white pepper

For the Sauerkraut

1 medium white cabbage, finely shredded
⅔ cup white wine
⅔ cup white wine vinegar

1 bouquet garni (2 teaspoons pickling spice, 2 teaspoons lightly crushed juniper berries, a pinch of thyme)
2 tablespoons unsalted butter
3 onions, sliced

To start the sauerkraut, place the shredded cabbage in a bowl with the wine and vinegar. Tie the bouquet garni ingredients in a square of muslin and add to the bowl. Leave to marinate for 48 hours, turning occasionally to make sure all the cabbage is marinated. This will give it a good pickly texture and taste.

Soak the bacon in water for 24 hours before boiling. Soaking the bacon releases excess salt content, leaving a better and less salty taste.

Once soaked, remove and wash the collar, and place in a pan with the vegetables, bay leaf and stock or water. Bring to the simmer and continue to simmer for 1-1½ hours. Once cooked, the bacon should be left to rest in the liquid for 20 minutes to relax the meat and make it more tender.

To make the mustard seed sauce, take 2½ cups of the cooking liquid and boil to reduce by half. Add the cream and cook for 10 minutes. Add the butter and mustard seed to taste. Check for seasoning with salt and pepper.

To finish the sauerkraut, drain off the liquid and keep to one side. Melt the butter in a pan and add the sliced onions. Allow to cook on a medium heat with no browning until slightly softened. Add the white cabbage, bouquet garni and 2–3 tablespoons of the liquid and cover with a lid. Cook on a medium heat, stirring from time to time. As the cabbage is cooking the pickling liquid will start to evaporate. Add some more liquid a little at a time until the cabbage becomes tender. This will take about 20 minutes. The cabbage should be tender but still have a slight bite. Season with salt and pepper.

To serve the dish, spoon some sauerkraut onto plates. Remove the bacon from the liquid and carve, allowing either one thick or two thinner slices per person. Sit the bacon on top of the cabbage and spoon some liquid over to add some extra moisture to the meat. The dish can now be finished with either extra liquid or the mustard seed cream sauce.

Boiled Collar of Bacon with Homemade Sauerkraut

Roast Leg of Pork

Roasting must be one of Britain's most popular cooking methods, especially on Sundays, and pork is a particular favorite. In fact it was one of the meats served at Christmas before turkeys were introduced from America.

Roast pork and applesauce is delicious if the pork has been cooked so that it stays succulent and the skin turns to crackling. You can also mix applesauce with cranberry sauce to eat with pork (or as a dip for the crackling). When I'm cooking pork I like to sit the leg on pork bones (if you can get them) to protect the meat, or you can use halved onions. The recipe of pork here serves at least 10 people but you can, of course, use a smaller cut to suit your own needs.

SERVES 10 or more

1 (8-10 lb) (3.5-4.5 kg) leg of pork	4 onions, halved
Lard or cooking oil	2½ cups Veal *Jus* (see p.224) or
Salt	alternative (see p.226)
Pork bones (optional)	Salt and freshly ground black pepper

Pre-heat the oven to 400°F (200°C).

To achieve a good, crisp crackling, the skin on the leg must be scored just deep enough to break through. Brush with lard or cooking oil and sprinkle fairly liberally with salt.

Sit the leg on a few pork bones in a roasting pan. Alternatively, sit the pork on halved onions with the skin left on, placing them face down. The onions not only protect the meat but also slowly cook, absorbing some of the pork juices. Leaving on the skins holds them together.

Roast the pork for about 20-30 minutes by which time the pork will have started coloring and crisping. Once it has reached the golden stage, loosely sit a piece of foil on top to prevent it from becoming too dark; don't overtighten it or the leg will create steam underneath and you won't get a crispy crackling. Roast for a further 3 hours, then remove the foil and finish cooking for about 30 minutes until the meat is tender and the crackling has crisped even more. Allow the meat to rest for 20-30 minutes before removing the crackling and carving the meat. A leg of pork this size will always take at least 4 hours to cook.

Once the pork has cooked, pour off any excess fat and add some gravy to collect all the taste from the cooking juices. The onion flavor comes through to lift the gravy. Spoon the onions out of their skins, season with salt and pepper and serve as a vegetable to go with the pork; they are packed with flavor.

Pork Crackling and Scratchings

Roast pork is delicious to eat, but I think the best bit is the crackling – good, crunchy, salted pork flavor.

To get good, crispy crackling, the skin has to be scored with a sharp knife just deep enough to break through. Brush the skin lightly with cooking oil or lard, then sprinkle liberally with salt before roasting. The salt will draw any water from the skin and leave a very crisp finish.

I also like to make crackling or scratchings without any meat attached (see overleaf). Ask the butcher for some pork rind, preferably from the loin, and cut off any excess fat underneath. Score and salt the skin and roast in a pre-heated oven at 400°F (200°C). The rind will take 30-40 minutes to become crunchy.

To make scratchings, instead of scoring the rind, remove the fat and cut it into ¼ inch (5 mm) strips, then sprinkle with salt. Bake in the pre-heated oven for about 30 minutes. It's nice to offer your own scratchings with pre-dinner drinks or use them in a starter for a meal. I like to make a pork scratching and apple salad. Simply quarter some apples and cut again into eight. Fry and toss them in butter, giving a little color, for 2-3 minutes. Sit them around the plate with warm pork scratchings and mix some snipped fresh chives with Basic Vinaigrette (see p.241) to spoon over. Dress the center of the plate with mixed salad leaves tossed in dressing.

If you've got some roast pork and crackling left over, use up the crackling in this salad. You can also spoon some Cranberry Sauce (see p.239) into the center of the plate, dressing the salad leaves on top.

OPPOSITE *Homemade Pork Scratchings in the foreground, and Crackling (see p.97).*

RIGHT *Seared Spicy Pork Belly (see p.100) served with Fried Spinach, Mushrooms and Bean Sprouts (see p.144).*

BELOW *Hocks and Hands (see p.101).*

Seared Spicy Pork Belly

Pork belly is a really cheap cut of meat and, I think, highly underrated. Belly slices are wonderful roasted or barbecued, they have a great balance of meat and pork fat content which helps them "crisp up" during cooking (see preceding page).

Well, for this recipe I'm not using the strips but instead squares of belly that have all bone and skin removed. It should be no problem to ask the butcher to cut some for you, but make sure they do remove all skin and bone. The squares you need should be about 3 inches (7.5 cm). Teriyaki marinade is available in most large supermarkets; you'll find it near the soy sauce. The pork almost tastes Chinese; it has a good spicy flavor and eats very well with just buttered noodles or with my Fried Spinach, Mushrooms and Bean Sprouts (see p.144).

SERVES 4

4 pork belly squares, prepared as above	4-5 tablespoons Basic Vinaigrette (see p.241)
1 tablespoon olive oil	
4 teaspoons clear honey	4-6 green onions

For the Spicy Marinade

⅔ cup teriyaki marinade	2 garlic cloves, sliced
⅓ cup soy sauce	6 tablespoons ginger root, finely diced or grated
1 teaspoon Tabasco sauce	
3 tablespoons Worcestershire sauce	

Score the pork belly squares diagonally on the fat side about ⅛ inch (3 mm) deep. They should also be scored very lightly underneath. The pork is now ready for marinating.

To make the marinade, simply mix all the ingredients together. Reserve 3 tablespoons to use in the finished dressing, then pour the rest over the pork, turning from time to time. The pork only needs to marinate for 24 hours before cooking. It can, of course, be left longer but this will increase the taste of the spices which could become too strong.

Pre-heat the oven to 400°F (200°C).

To cook the pork, heat the olive oil in a roasting pan and add the pork fat-side-down over a medium heat. The fat will start to color almost immediately, giving a rich roasted/seared color. Continue to color until quite dark. Turn the pork and cook in the pre-heated oven for about 15-20 minutes. The cooking time will really depend on the thickness of the belly.

Once cooked, spoon the honey on top and glaze under a hot broiler. Remove the pork and leave to rest for a few minutes. Mix any excess honey in the pan with the reserved marinade and the vinaigrette dressing and strain through a sieve. Cut the green onions into small, thin oval pieces. Slice the pork into thin slices and sit in the bowl. Spoon the marinade dressing over and sprinkle with the green onions.

Knuckles and Hocks, Hands and Scrag Ends

Knuckle, hocks and hands of pork or lamb scrag ends are all "rough" cuts of meat. Although cheap, they are are packed with flavor, especially when slow roasted and served with gravy (see p.99).

Any of these cuts can be roasted in a medium oven at about 350°F (180°C) for 2-2½ hours.

Hand of pork (from the shoulder with the trotter removed) can be bought on or off the bone. Once scored and tied, it is ready to cook. If it's salted and slowly roasted, you will have some very crispy crackling and moist pork underneath. Sliced and served with mustard or applesauce, it tastes delicious. It's a brilliant cut to roast and just sit and pick at, or break off crackling, tear the meat and eat it in a French baguette sandwich with the bread soaking up all the juices. The same can be done with the other cuts.

Scrag ends of lamb are normally casseroled, but a knuckle is for roasting and eats well if glazed with honey and mint.

These are cuts of meat we should use more often. If you have four knuckles of lamb roasted off for a dinner and you sit them in a bowl and plonk them on the table, I promise you everyone will be excited and delighted by the messy eating!

Breast of Lamb with a Mustard and Herb Crust

Breast of lamb is a cut of meat taken from the belly. It's quite cheap and is packed with flavor. When buying lamb breasts, make sure the lamb has been boned and any excess fat has been removed. One breast will give you enough for two portions. Once cut in two, roll the lamb lengthwise and tie tightly. Lamb breasts are usually roasted or cut into chunks and braised. This dish holds several cooking methods: frying, braising and broiling. It's braised in a stock and can be cooked a few days in advance and kept in its jellied stock. You can add any lamb bones to the stock during cooking to increase the lamb flavor.

SERVES 4

2 de-boned lamb breasts, each cut in half to give you 4 portions, rolled and tied	2 celery stalks, diced
2 tablespoons lamb fat or cooking oil	½ leek, diced
4 tablespoons unsalted butter	4-6 cups Chicken Stock (see p.222)
1 garlic clove, crushed	A few lamb bones (optional)
1 sprig of fresh thyme	1 teaspoon chopped mixed thyme, sage and rosemary
1 sprig of fresh rosemary	1 recipe Basic Crumble Mix (see p.114)
A few fresh sage leaves	⅔ cup heavy whipping double cream
1 onion, diced	2-4 teaspoons Dijon or stone-ground mustard
2 carrots, diced	

Heat a frying pan and brown the lamb breasts in the fat or oil. Melt half the butter in a large casserole or roasting pan and fry the garlic, herbs and vegetables slowly for a few minutes. Add the stock and lamb bones, if using. Bring to the simmer. Add the lamb breasts and simmer until tender; this will take about 2 hours.

Once cooked, the lamb can be left in the stock and jellied (to use later) or taken out of the stock and finished with the crust.

Add the chopped mixed herbs to the crumble mix and flavor with 1-2 teaspoons of mustard.

Cut the meat into ½ inch (1 cm) slices and separate into portions. Push the slices together, just slightly parted at an angle. Top with the herb crust and crisp under a hot broiler until golden brown.

To make the sauce, reduce some of the cooking liquid to about 1¼ cups. Thicken with the remaining butter and add the heavy whipping cream, cooking for 5-10 minutes, then add 1-2 teaspoons of mustard and serve.

Breast of Lamb with a Mustard and Herb Crust.

Roast Rack of Lamb with a Parsnip Crumble

The rack of lamb can be ordered from your butcher. It is actually the fillet of lamb with the bones attached. If you cut between the bones, this gives you lamb cutlets, and although you can use cutlets for this recipe, I prefer to leave the meat on the bone or as whole fillets before roasting; this will give a totally different taste and texture to the meat. Ask for the lamb to be French-trimmed and all fat removed; this means that the bones are clean. You now have the two meat fillets with individual bones attached. Split both through the middle leaving four roasting joints with about three bones attached on each (any excess bones can be cut off).

SERVES 4

2 racks of lamb, French-trimmed and
    fat removed
Salt and freshly ground black pepper
1 tablespoon cooking fat

1 recipe Parsnip Crumble (see p.117)
1¼ cups Red Wine Sauce (see p.230)

Pre-heat the oven to 400°F (200°C).

Season the meat with salt and pepper, then brown it in the cooking fat in a hot pan on top of the stove. Once colored, transfer to a roasting pan in the pre-heated oven and roast until medium rare. This will take 8-10 minutes, longer if you prefer the lamb a little more cooked. To test the meat, simply press between thumb and forefinger; the meat should feel tender and just give when pressure is applied. The lamb should now be left to rest for about 10 minutes before carving and serving, as this will give the meat a softer texture.

Meanwhile, shape the crumbles in individual 4 inch (10 cm) pastry cutter rings (see p.117). Finish in the hot oven or under the broiler until golden and crunchy.

Carve between the bones, giving three roasted cutlets per portion. Sit the lamb on top of the individual parsnip crumbles and pour the red wine sauce around.

Roast Rack of Lamb with a Leek and Mustard Crumble

Here is another way of serving rack of lamb. It's simple to cook. Just follow the lamb preparation and cooking instructions on p.104.

Racks of lamb also eat well and cook a little quicker if the meat is off the bone. Providing that the lamb is French-trimmed, you can simply cut the meat away from the bone, leaving lamb fillets. Once cooked, these can be sliced either across or lengthwise.

The Leek and Mustard Crumble works very well as part of the main dish or as a separate vegetable accompaniment.

SERVES 4

2 racks of lamb, French-trimmed and
    fat removed
1 recipe Leek and Mustard Crumble
    (see p.116)

1¼ cups Red Wine Sauce (see p.230)

Roast the lamb (see p.104) and prepare and cook the crumbles in individual pastry cutter rings (see p.119). Arrange the crumbles on a serving plate and sit the roast lamb on top. Pour the red wine sauce around.

Peppered Lamb Fillet with Mint and Caper Sauce

The pepper flavor works really well with the sweetness of lamb, without being overpowering. This dish is packed with lots of different flavors, all of which you can still identify and taste. I use a standard pepper mill to grind the peppercorns, then shake them through a sieve to keep out any large pieces. The lamb fillet I use is from the rack of lamb, which is the joint lamb cutlets come from. All I've done is take the meat completely off the bone.

You don't have to follow this recipe exactly. The same idea can be used for roasting a leg of lamb. Roll it in the pepper and roast it as normal. When the joint is carved, every slice will have a wonderful pepper taste. You can make the same sauce or just flavor your lamb gravy with mint and capers.

Spinach eats very well with this dish, as do Fondant Potatoes (see p.134), which help to mop up the sauce.

SERVES 4

2 racks of lamb, filleted

Black or white peppercorns, crushed
and sieved

Salt and freshly ground black pepper

1 tablespoon cooking oil or fat

For the Sauce (serves 8-10)

1 large shallot or ½ onion, roughly
chopped

1 carrot, roughly chopped

1 celery stalk, roughly chopped

1 tablespoon unsalted butter

12 fresh mint leaves

1½ –2¼ cups red wine

2½ cups Veal *Jus* (see p.224) or
alternative (see p.226)

1 bay leaf

2 teaspoons small capers

Pre-heat the oven to 425°F (220°C).

To make the sauce, cook the vegetables and bay leaf in the butter until softened and lightly colored. Add the mint and wine and boil to reduce by three-quarters. Add the *jus* or gravy, bring to the boil and simmer gently for 20 minutes. Season with salt and pepper and strain. The sauce should have a mint flavor. Add the capers just before serving.

Meanwhile, cut the fillets in half, giving you four individual portions. Roll them in the crushed peppercorns, shaking off any excess. Season with salt. Heat a roasting pan with the oil or fat and fry the lamb for 1-2 minutes, sealing and browning all over. Finish the lamb in the pre-heated oven for about 6-8 minutes to cook the lamb to medium. If you want the meat rarer, cook for 5 minutes, or allow 10-12 minutes if you like it well done.

Always allow meat to rest for 5-10 minutes once it is cooked; this will make it more tender to eat. Carve the meat and serve it with the caper *jus*.

Variations

You can make the sauce without the vegetables, just by reducing the red wine with the mint, then adding the *jus*.

Peppered Lamb Fillet with Mint and Caper Sauce
served with Fondant Potatoes (see p.134).

Stewed Venison with Vegetables in Red Wine

Venison (deer meat) for stewing should come from the haunch, or you can use neck. I like to cut the meat into large pieces rather than dice. It takes a little longer to cook but the texture and taste are wonderful.

SERVES 4

2 lb (900 g) haunch of venison	A few black peppercorns, lightly
1 tablespoon cooking fat or oil	crushed
1 lb (450 g) onions, sliced	3 cups red wine
1 sprig of fresh thyme	3¾-5 cups Veal *Jus* (p.224) or alternative
1 bay leaf	(see p.226)
A few juniper berries, lightly crushed	Salt and freshly ground black pepper

For the Garnish

8-10 oz (225-275 g) pearl onions	4 celery stalks
1 tablespoon cooking fat	6 large mushrooms
3 carrots	

Cut the venison into chunks and brown in the fat in a hot frying pan until completely sealed; remove from the pan. Cook the onions with the thyme, bay leaf, juniper berries and peppercorns for a few minutes. Add half the red wine and boil to reduce until almost dry. Add the *jus* and venison, bring to the simmer, then cook gently for 1½-2 hours, skimming occasionally. Add a tablespoon or two of water if the sauce becomes too thick.

When the stew is almost ready, fry the onions until well colored. While they are coloring, quarter the carrots lengthwise, then cut at an angle into ¾ inch (2 cm) pieces. Slice the celery and quarter the mushrooms. Remove the onions from the pan. Add the carrots and celery and brown lightly. Add them to the onions. Add the mushrooms to the pan and fry for a few minutes, then return all the vegetables to the pan and cover with the remaining wine. Boil to reduce until almost dry. The vegetables should now be cooked.

Remove the meat from the sauce and strain the sauce through a sieve. Return the meat to the sauce and check for seasoning with salt and pepper. Add the vegetables to the meat and serve the dish as a stew, or sit the meat in bowls and top with the braised vegetables with the sauce spooned over.

Variations

To enrich the stew red currant jelly can be added to sweeten the sauce; or a spoonful of Dijon or English mustard or a dash of Worcestershire sauce.

The dish can also be turned into a pie by spooning the stew into a pie dish and topping with Shortcrust Pastry (see p.211) or Puff Pastry (see p.212).

You can adapt the recipe to use pheasant, grouse or other game birds.

Another venison dish I enjoy is roasted loin cooked pink, then carved and set on top of a basic potato and vegetable dish, like Bubble and Squeak (see p.118) or Beet Bubble and Squeak (see p.140). Pour some Red Wine Sauce (see p.230) around and the dish is ready.

Venison also eats well with Celeriac and Potato Dauphinoise (see p.136).

Venison Dumplings

You can make these dumplings to serve with the Stewed Venison (see p.108). The offal will give a good, strong, gamey flavor, but if you're not too keen on offal, replace it with 6 oz (175 g) finely chopped or minced black pudding sausage. This will give a strong flavor and can be used in so many other stews or braised dishes, with pork, chicken, duck or lamb.

SERVES 4

2 oz (50 g) venison heart, coarsely minced
2 oz (50 g) venison liver, coarsely minced
2 oz (50 g) venison kidney, coarsely minced
2 tablespoons finely chopped onion, cooked in butter
½ teaspoon chopped fresh sage and thyme

4 oz (100 g) shredded suet
1¾ cups self-rising flour
4–5 juniper berries, crushed
A pinch of salt
¼–⅓ cup water
1 egg
1¼ cups Chicken Stock (see p.222) or water

Mix the heart, liver and kidney with the chopped onions, herbs, suet, flour, juniper berries and salt. Mix with the water and egg to a reasonably firm dough. Roll into balls and poach in stock or water for 20 minutes. The dumplings can then be added to a stew.

Homemade Corned Beef

You may be surprised to find that this really is a simple recipe. It just needs a little advanced planning as the beef must be soaked for three days before cooking. Corned beef is readily available for everyone, but it's so good to eat it homemade. The texture is similar to a standard corned beef, but this recipe isn't quite as pink in color. The pig's trotters are optional but will help to create a jelly in the cooking liquid.

Corned beef is lovely to eat with chutney for tea or supper, or to break into pieces to make corned beef hash, fried with onions and potatoes. Hash is good for a cooked breakfast or lunch/supper dish.

The recipe I'm giving is using 5 lb (2.25 kg) of beef. This can be cut down in half but any smaller quantities won't really give you the right balance of beef meat and fat.

Serves 8

5 lb (2.25 kg) beef flank	2 pig's trotters (optional)
7½ cups cold water	2 tablespoons gelatin powder (optional)
¼–⅓ cup salt	

Trim the beef flank of all visible sinews but leave it as a whole piece. Mix the water and ¼ cup of salt to create brine. To test the strength of the brine, sit a raw new potato in the water; the potato should float. If it won't float, simply add the remaining salt, or more if needed. Sit the beef in the brine and chill for 3 days.

Remove the meat from the brine and wash it, discarding the salt water. Sit the meat in a clean pan with the pig's trotters, if using. Top up with fresh water. Bring to the boil, then simmer for 2½–3 hours, skimming any impurities from the liquid.

Once cooked, remove the meat from the liquid. Drain the cooking liquid through a fine sieve and taste; it should have a good beef flavor. Discard the trotters, if using. Bring the stock to the boil and boil to reduce in volume, and increase its flavor and jelly content. Test the stock/jelly by spooning onto a small plate and placing in the refrigerator. The jelly must set very firm to enable it to hold the beef together. If it doesn't set firm enough, then add some or all of the gelatin to the mix. Only about 2½–3¾ cups of finished jelly stock will be needed. Make sure you do test the stock/jelly first as the dish is better if only set using natural jellies.

While the beef is still warm, break it down into pieces. The meat will almost separate itself between sinew strips. Any excess sinew can be removed, but make sure that all fat content is kept. The meat can now be pushed through a large grinder plate (¼–½ inch/ 5-10 mm) or chopped by hand with the fat. Mix the meat with 2½ cups of reduced liquid and check the consistency. The meat should absorb the liquid and be left reasonably loose. If the mix is too firm, add another 1¼ cups of stock. Taste the corned beef before setting in a mold and correct the seasoning with salt and pepper. The mix can now be pressed firmly into a terrine mold or bowl and set in the refrigerator overnight.

Once set, turn out the corned beef and serve with a salad and pickle, fried for breakfast or turn it into a corned beef hash.

Homemade Corned Beef.

Ox Cheek Stew with Neeps and Tatties

Ox cheeks are an unusual cut of beef with a good, open texture which is ideal for braising or stewing as it enables the beef to absorb all the sauce and liquid. If you can't find a butcher to offer you the cheeks, then just use large pieces of chuck steak. This is similar in texture and will work well in this recipe.

"Neeps and Tatties" are British slang for turnips and potatoes.

SERVES 4-6

2½-3 lb (1.1-1.5 kg) ox cheeks, trimmed of all fat and sinew
Salt and freshly ground black pepper
2 tablespoons cooking fat
2 large onions, sliced
1 small garlic clove, crushed
1 sprig of fresh thyme

1 bay leaf
3 cups red wine
3¾-5 cups Veal *Jus* (see p.224) or alternative (see p.226)
1 lb (450 g) shallots
2 tablespoons unsalted butter

For the Neeps and Tatties

1 lb (450 g) turnips
1 lb (450 g) potatoes

½ cup (8 tablespoons) unsalted butter

Season the ox cheeks with salt and pepper. Pre-heat a frying pan and add a little cooking fat. Fry the cheeks until well browned on all sides. Remove from the pan and drain off excess fat or liquid. Brown the sliced onions in a large casserole or roasting pan until well colored. Add the garlic, thyme, bay leaf and half the red wine. Bring to the boil and boil to reduce until almost dry. Add the veal *jus* and ox cheeks and bring to the simmer. Braise the cheeks slowly for 1½-2 hours until tender.

While the cheeks are cooking, split the peeled shallots in half lengthwise and cook in a very little butter until well colored (almost burnt). Add the remaining red wine and reduce until almost dry.

Meanwhile, cook the turnips and potatoes separately in boiling salted water until tender. (I also like to add carrots to this recipe which gives a slightly sweeter flavor.) Drain and leave to dry for a few minutes. Lightly mash the vegetables or stir with a wooden spoon to give a coarse purée. If you prefer a smoother finish push the vegetables through a sieve. Add the butter and season with salt and pepper.

Once the cheeks are cooked, remove them from the sauce and drain the sauce through a sieve. Re-heat the cheeks in the finished sauce and spoon into serving bowls. The shallots can be mixed with the stew or sat on top to finish. Serve with the turnips and potatoes.

Vegetarian Dishes

I often find that vegetarian dishes are either not given enough thought or far too much, and are totally overdone with too many garnishes. My feelings about all dishes are that nothing should be added unless it's going to enhance the flavors.

All our eating habits and moods change. Whenever I have a "pub lunch" (not often enough!) I always go for the vegetarian dish of the day. It's usually a vegetable cottage pie, pasta dish or quiche, and I always enjoy it.

A quiche is easy and simple to make, so I decided to make a feature with vegetarian tarts all using the same base mixture. The scope is endless; so many different flavors can be added to give totally different results. Another dish that also has a lot of variety is a vegetarian crumble; these can be complete meals on their own or accompaniments to a main course dish.

Basic Crumble Mix

This recipe really couldn't be simpler. It's just two ingredients held together with butter and, of course, seasoned with salt and pepper. The nicest thing about it is that it lends itself to so many flavor combinations: from parsley and lemon to horseradish or mustard and herbs. If you are using additional flavors, add them before stirring in the shallot butter. All these flavors work well with fish, meat or vegetarian dishes.

It's best to use sliced bread that is 24 hours old, as this will firm the bread slightly and prevent the crumbs from becoming doughy.

SERVES 4

6-8 slices white bread
2-4 tablespoons unsalted butter, melted
2 large shallots or ½ onion, finely
    chopped

Salt and freshly ground black pepper

Remove and discard the crusts from the bread and cut into quarters. The quickest way to turn these slices into crumbs is to process in a food processor. If you don't have a food processor, simply push the slices through a metal sieve.

Melt the butter with the chopped shallots and bring to the simmer, remove from the heat and leave to cool.

Gradually spoon some of the shallot butter into the crumbs, mixing all the time. The mix will be ready when it holds once pressed together, but it should stay free-flowing.

Use the crumble as directed in the individual recipes.

Spinach and Horseradish Crumble

This crumble recipe has the sharp tang of horseradish which goes so well with the buttered spinach. I've used this with lots of dishes, especially roast meats, grilled herrings or salmon.

SERVES 4

1 recipe Basic Crumble Mix (see p.114)	2 lb (900 g) fresh spinach, washed
2 tablespoons horseradish sauce	Salt and freshly ground white pepper
2-4 tablespoons unsalted butter	Freshly grated nutmeg (optional)

Follow the recipe for the basic crumble, only using a maximum of 2 tablespoons of butter. Mix the horseradish sauce with the crust mix and taste, adding a little more if you like a stronger taste.

Cook the spinach at the last moment for the maximum taste, and cook it quickly. Heat a large, shallow pan and add the butter. As soon as the butter is bubbling, add the spinach, increasing the heat. Stir lightly with a wooden spoon to ensure even cooking. The leaves will immediately start to break down and will be cooked within 1-2 minutes. Season with salt, pepper and nutmeg, if using. If the spinach has produced a lot of liquid, drain it into a small pan and boil to reduce, then return it to the spinach. Spoon the spinach into a large buttered baking dish and cover with the crumble mix. Finish under the broiler until golden brown.

Variations

Herbs can be added to the crumbs: parsley, tarragon, thyme or sage will all work well.

You can reserve the spinach liquid and purée in a little butter with a food processor or blender to create a spinach butter sauce. This works well with grilled herrings.

It is best to make this dish at the last minute, but there is an alternative. Plunge the spinach into boiling salted water for about 1-2 minutes until just tender, then drain and refresh in ice-cold water. Squeeze any excess water from the spinach, add a tablespoon of softened butter and season with salt, pepper and nutmeg. Spoon into an ovenproof, microwave baking dish and cover with the crust mix. Before serving, re-heat the whole dish in the microwave, then brown and crisp under the broiler.

Leek and Mustard Crumble on Cheesy Mashed Potatoes

This recipe can be adapted to so many dishes, plus it's a complete vegetarian meal on its own. You can even make it without the cheesy mashed potatoes and still have a great accompaniment to many simple meat or fish dishes.

SERVES 4-6

½ cup (8 tablespoons) unsalted butter
2 onions, sliced
⅔ cup Vegetable Stock (see p.223)
1-1½ lb (450-675 g) leeks, split and
    sliced
2 teaspoons chopped fresh parsley
2 teaspoons chopped fresh tarragon

1 recipe Basic Crumble Mix (see p.114)
2 teaspoons stone-ground mustard
2-3 cups or ½ recipe Mashed Potatoes
    (see p.133)
1½-3 cups Cheddar, grated
Salt and freshly ground white pepper

Pre-heat the oven to 400°F (200°C).

Melt 2 tablespoons of butter in a pan. When the butter begins to bubble, add the sliced onions and cook for a few minutes over a medium heat until slightly softened. Add the stock and bring to the boil. Add the leeks, return to the boil and cook for 30 seconds. Strain off the leeks and onions, keeping the stock. Boil the stock until reduced by half to increase its flavor.

To finish the crumble mix, add the chopped parsley and tarragon to the mix, then add the stone-ground mustard to taste.

Warm the mashed potatoes with 1½ cups of the grated Cheddar until melted. I prefer the cheese flavor to be stronger, so continue to stir in the cheese until you have the flavor you want. Check for seasoning with salt and pepper.

Spoon the mashed potatoes into a large baking dish. Warm the onions and leeks in a teaspoon of the vegetable liquid, then spoon over the potatoes, and finish with the mustard seed crumble mix. Finish in the pre-heated oven or under a hot broiler for about 10 minutes until the crumble is golden and crunchy.

To make the sauce, re-heat the reduced vegetable liquid and vigorously whisk in the remaining butter to give an almost creamy consistency. Purée the liquid and butter together in a food processor or blender; this will really bind the sauce. Season with salt and pepper and serve with the crumble.

Variations

Try different cheeses instead of the Cheddar; a smoked cheese tastes good.

The filling can also be left to cool and chilled and either re-heated through in the oven or microwaved.

Parsnip Crumble

If you want to make this in individual portions, divide the parsnips between four or six (4 inch) (10 cm) buttered pastry cutter rings, pushing the parsnips in so they almost mold together.

SERVES 4-6

2 lb (900 g) parsnips
2 tablespoons unsalted butter or cooking fat
Salt and freshly ground black pepper

1 recipe Basic Crumble Mix (see p.114)
1 teaspoon chopped fresh thyme
1 teaspoon chopped fresh rosemary

Pre-heat the oven to 425°F (220°C).

Peel and split the parsnips lengthwise into quarters, and cut out the woody centers. To roast the parsnips, pre-heat a baking sheet on top of the stove with a little butter or cooking fat. Add the parsnips and cook until golden brown. Season with salt and pepper. Roast in the pre-heated oven for 15-20 minutes, turning occasionally for even color and cooking. For this particular dish, the parsnips need to be slightly overcooked to help shape them into the pastry rings and also give the center a purée texture while the outside remains crispy.

To make the crumble, add the herbs to the crumbs before molding with the shallot/onion butter. Spoon the crumble over the top of the parsnips in the large baking dish or individual rings and finish in the hot oven or under a hot broiler until golden and crunchy.

If you wish to make individual crumbles, place the buttered pastry cutter rings onto a greased baking sheet and divide the parsnips between them, pressing firmly so they will mold together. Spoon the crumble over the top of each one and finish in the hot oven or under a hot broiler until golden. To serve, remove the rings from the hot crumble and arrange on plates.

Roast Parsnip and Chestnut Crumble on Bubble and Squeak

Bubble and Squeak is a classic British dish that gets its name from the noise it makes when it's cooking. It's a very popular dish on pub menus. This version makes a great alternative vegetarian Christmas lunch that includes all those familiar traditional flavors (see p. 63). It can be eaten on its own, or you can use this recipe as your total accompaniment to roast turkey. It can also be made any time of the year (perhaps leaving out the chestnuts!).

You can buy cooked chestnuts in cans or frozen. If you are using fresh chestnuts in shell, you will need about 8 oz (225 g). Pre-heat the broiler. Pierce the chestnuts once with a knife, then place under the broiler for about 15 minutes until the skins split. Leave to cool, then peel and chop roughly.

This dish eats very well with cranberry sauce, especially my recipe flavored with orange and port (see p.239).

I like to make this in individual 4 inch (10cm) pastry cutter rings, but if you don't have them, don't worry. It works just as well and looks really tasty in a large baking dish. Just make the bubble and squeak in the traditional way in a large frying pan, browning on both sides, and then spooning into the large baking dish in the same way.

If you have decided to make this in advance and have chilled it before finishing with the crumble, then it's best to re-heat in the oven for 30 minutes before adding the crumble. Return the dish to the oven or broiler until it turns golden brown.

SERVES 4

For the Parsnips

1 tablespoon unsalted butter
2 tablespoons cooking oil
2½ lb (1.1 kg) peeled parsnips, split into
    quarters lengthwise and cored

Salt and freshly ground black pepper
1 tablespoons clear honey (optional)

For the Bubble and Squeak

1½ lb (675 g) Brussels sprouts
4 tablespoons unsalted butter
2 large onions, thinly sliced

3 cups or ½ recipe Mashed Potatoes (see
    p.133), made without milk or cream

For the Crumble

2 tablespoons unsalted butter
1 large onion, finely chopped
4-6 oz (100-175 g) cooked chestnuts,
    chopped (optional)
2 tablespoons chopped fresh parsley
2 tablespoons chopped fresh sage

1 tablespoon chopped fresh thyme
3 cups fresh white breadcrumbs

Watercress sprigs to garnish
1 recipe Vegetable Butter Sauce (see
    p.228) to serve

Pre-heat the oven to 400°F (200°C) and grease a baking sheet.

Heat the butter and oil in a roasting pan on top of the stove, add the parsnips and fry on a medium heat, turning the parsnips until golden. Season with salt and pepper, then transfer to the pre-heated oven and roast for 15-20 minutes. The parsnips will now be deep golden brown and crispy, but almost overcooked and soft inside. While still hot, lightly toss in the honey, if using.

To make the bubble and squeak, cook the sprouts in boiling salted water until tender. Cool and refresh in cold water. Once cold, halve lengthwise and slice. In a small pan, melt 2 tablespoons of butter and gently cook the onions for 4-5 minutes until softened. Leave to cool. Mix the onions with the sprouts, then add the mashed potatoes a spoonful at a time until a firm texture is achieved. Season with salt and pepper.

If you wish to make these into individual crumbles, grease four to six 4 inch (10 cm) pastry cutter rings and divide the mix between them. Heat the remaining butter in a frying pan and with a sturdy spatula place the filled pastry cutter rings in the pan and fry until golden brown underneath; this will take 4-5 minutes. Once ready, transfer again with a sturdy spatula, the filled rings onto the greased baking sheet, cooked-side-down. Spoon the cooked parsnips on top of the bubble and squeak, lightly pressing down. You can leave the recipe to cool then chill at this stage and finish before serving.

To make the crumble (almost a Christmas stuffing), heat the butter in a small pan and cook the onion over a medium heat for 2-3 minutes. In a large bowl mix the chestnuts, chopped herbs and crumbs and season with salt and pepper. Add the onion and butter and mix together.

Sprinkle the crumble mix on top of the warm potatoes and Brussels sprouts and parsnips and place in the pre-heated oven for 10-12 minutes (double the time if it has been chilled). The dish should now be hot all the way through and can be finished under a hot broiler until golden and crunchy. Remove the rings from the hot crumble and arrange the bubble and squeak on plates, garnish with watercress and serve with the vegetable butter sauce.

Savory Tarts

I could make this almost a separate chapter; the combinations go on and on. These tarts make perfect vegetarian dishes as well as just good starters, main courses or snacks. They have a different texture to traditional quiche lorraine and are very easy to make. You can make this in one large tart pan or as individual tartlets.

The basic tart mix is made up of eggs, cream and cheese. I am using grated fresh Parmesan to give a good, strong flavor and a smooth consistency. Other cheese can be used, from Cheddar and Gruyère to a smoked cheese – Italian Pecorino works well. When cooking the tart mix, it's important not to let it boil or this will scramble the eggs.

You can use puff or shortcrust pastry for your tarts, both of which are available at most supermarkets. I prefer puff pastry as it gives a lighter, cleaner finish. Turn to p.212 for details on how to make and bake blind puff pastry shells.

Basic Tart Mix

This recipe has almost unlimited combinations. It also has to be one of the quickest and easiest tart mixes to make. The quantity of this basic recipe can easily be adjusted, it really depends on what the filling is going to be. This amount will be enough for 6 (4 inch) (10 cm) individual or 1 (10 inch) (25 cm) tart.

SERVES 6

1¼ cups heavy whipping cream	Salt and freshly ground black pepper
2 heaped tablespoons freshly grated Parmesan	2 eggs, beaten

Beat the cream, eggs and Parmesan and season with salt and pepper. The mix is now ready to use.

Almost any filling can be bound and finished with this mix, but all the fillings must be previously cooked or blanched before adding to the Parmesan cream. The filling can then be warmed until it thickens, making sure it does not boil as this will scramble the eggs. The mixture can then be spooned into pastry crusts and cooked in the oven until set, or chilled to be used later.

Onion and Mushroom Tart with Parsley Garlic Crust

This tart cooks almost like a crumble with the garlic and parsley crust (see overleaf).
It eats very well with a tomato salad or Tomato and Mustard Seed Salad (see p.126).

Serves 6

2 tablespoons unsalted butter
1 tablespoon olive oil
4 onions, sliced
3 cups sliced button mushrooms,
Salt and freshly ground black pepper
1 recipe Basic Tart Mix (see p.120)

6 (4 inch) (10 cm) or 1 (10 inch) (25 cm)
    Puff Pastry crusts, blind baked (see
    p.212)
½ recipe Basic Crumble Mix (see p.114)
2 tablespoons chopped fresh parsley
1 large garlic clove

Pre-heat the oven to 400°F (200°C).

Melt the butter with the olive oil, add the sliced onions and cook over a moderate heat for 2-3 minutes. Add the button mushrooms, increasing the heat, and cook for a further 2-3 minutes. Season with salt and pepper. Add the basic tart mix and cook without boiling for 15-20 minutes. The filling is now ready to use, or it can also be cooled and kept chilled for a few days.

Spoon the mix into the cooked pastry crusts and finish in the pre-heated oven for 15-20 minutes. One large tart will need 30-35 minutes.

While the tart is cooking, start to make the crumble topping. Add the crushed garlic to the shallots in the original recipe and cook in the butter. Add the chopped parsley to the breadcrumbs and finish as per recipe.

Once the tarts are cooked, sprinkle the parsley and garlic crust on top, covering the tart completely. Finish slowly under a broiler until golden and crispy.

Clockwise, starting top left: Onion and Mushroom Tart
with a Parsley Garlic Crust (see above); Parsley, Shallot and Onion Tart
with Tomato and Mustard Seed Salad (see p.126); Ratatouille Tart
with Crispy Eggplant and Tomato Dressing (see p.127);
Wild Mushroom Tart (see p. 125);
Provençale Tart (see p.124).

Provençale Tart

This is similar to the Ratatouille Tart (see p.127), using onions, zucchini, red and green peppers, but they both eat very differently with different textures, tastes and sauces. You can make the filling in advance and keep in the refrigerator for a few days. The tart eats very well with a pesto mayonnaise sauce (see preceding pages).

SERVES 6

2 tablespoons unsalted butter
2 onions, sliced
1 large red bell pepper, sliced
1 large green bell pepper, sliced
1 garlic clove, crushed
1 recipe Basic Tart Mix (see p.120)

2 zucchini, sliced
1-2 tablespoons olive oil
4-5 plum tomatoes, sliced
6 (4 inch) (10 cm) or 1 (10 inch) (25 cm) Puff Pastry crusts, baked blind (see p.212)

For the Sauce

1 tablespoon Pesto Sauce (see p.235)

⅔ cup Mayonnaise (see p.242)

Pre-heat the oven to 400°F (200°C).

Melt the butter in a pan and add the onions, peppers and garlic. Season with salt and pepper and cook for 4-5 minutes over a moderate heat until the vegetables begin to soften. Add the basic tart mix and warm through gently until the mix thickens; this will take 15-20 minutes. Do not allow the mix to boil.

Fry the zucchini slices in a hot frying pan in a little olive oil for 20-30 seconds, giving the zucchini some color. Spoon the filling into the puff pastry crust or crusts, then decorate the top of the tarts with slices of zucchini and tomato, making two alternating lines of each. Cook in the pre-heated oven for 15-20 minutes for individual tarts or 30-35 minutes for one tart until it sets to the touch. If the mix has been chilled it will take an extra 8-10 minutes to cook.

Mix the pesto with the mayonnaise and check seasoning with salt and pepper. Spoon the mixture onto the center of the plates or bowls and sit the tart on top. Finish with a trickle of olive oil.

Note

The quantity of pesto to mayonnaise is only a guideline – more pesto can be added for a stronger taste. Shop-bought pesto and mayonnaise can be used.

Wild Mushroom Tart

Wild mushrooms are becoming increasingly readily available in grocery stores and supermarkets. The variety also seems to be growing. Oyster mushrooms, ceps, trompettes de la mort and chanterelles can all be used in this tart, as a mixture or just using one type.

If you can't find fresh wild mushrooms, you should have no problems locating some dried wild mushrooms. These just have to be soaked in cold water until they soften, then you can use them as the fresh ones. Keep the soaking water, sieve it to remove any impurities, then boil it until reduced. This soaking liquid will increase the wild mushroom flavors.

The tart eats very well with a green salad and a dressing made with olive oil and chopped black olives and chives (see pp. 122-23).

SERVES 6

2 cups sliced button mushrooms
6 oz (175 g) fresh wild mushrooms OR
    4 oz (100 g) soaked dried wild
    mushrooms
2 tablespoons unsalted butter
2 tablespoons olive oil

2 large onions, sliced
1 small garlic clove
1 recipe Basic Tart Mix (see p.120)
6 (4 inch) (10 cm) or 1 (10 in) (25cm)
    Puff Pastry crusts, blind baked (see
    p.212)

Pre-heat the oven to 400°F (200°C).

Fresh wild mushrooms must be washed and cleaned. If you are using oyster mushrooms, these can be torn by hand into strips. Any large mushrooms should be trimmed and sliced. If you are using dried mushrooms, soak them until soft, then drain.

Melt the butter with 1 tablespoon of olive oil in a large pan. Add the onions and cook for a few minutes without coloring. Add the garlic and mushrooms. Increase the heat and stir for a few minutes. If some liquid has formed from the mushrooms with the onions, drain off any excess liquid to a separate pan and boil until reduced.

Add the mushroom and onion mix to the basic tart mix with any reduced liquid. Warm and thicken the tart mix for 15-20 minutes over a low heat, without overheating or boiling. Spoon the mix into the pastry crusts and finish in the pre-heated oven for 20 minutes for individual tarts or 30-35 minutes for one tart. Once cooked and just set, brush with the remaining olive oil and serve.

Parsley, Shallot and Onion Tart with Tomato and Mustard Seed Salad

Flatleaf parsley has more flavor than ordinary parsley. It looks similar to cilantro. If you can't find any, just use ordinary parsley. You can make one tart or six individual ones (see pp. 122–23).

SERVES 6

6 (4 inch) (10 cm) or 1 (10 inch) (25 cm) Puff Pastry crusts, blind baked (see p.212)
1 large bunch of flatleaf parsley
1 tablespoon olive oil
2 tablespoons unsalted butter

3 large onions, sliced
8 oz (225 g) shallots, sliced
1 garlic clove, crushed
1 recipe Basic Tart Mix (see p.120)
Salt and freshly ground white pepper

For the Salad

6 ripe plum tomatoes
1 teaspoon stone-ground mustard or to taste

4 tablespoons Basic Vinaigrette (see p.241)
1 teaspoon snipped fresh chives

Pre-heat the oven to 400°F (200°C).

Pick the flatleaf parsley from the stalks and blanch in boiling salted water for 45 seconds. Drain and refresh with cold water. Squeeze out any excess water from the parsley and lightly chop.

To cook the onions and shallots, warm the olive oil and butter until the butter begins to bubble. Add the onions, shallots and garlic and cook over a moderate heat without coloring until softened. Remove from the heat and allow to cool. Once cooled, mix with the chopped parsley and the basic tart mix. Season with salt and pepper. Warm the tart mix through gently until thickened.

Spoon the tart mix into the pastry crusts and bake in the pre-heated oven for 30–35 minutes for one tart or 15-20 minutes for individual tarts.

To make the salad, core the tomatoes and cut into eight pieces. Season with salt and pepper. Add the mustard to the basic dressing, then add the snipped chives. Mix the dressing with the salad and serve with the warm tart.

Ratatouille Tart with Crispy Eggplant and Tomato Dressing

We all like ratatouille; it has that Italian theme and is packed with different flavors. Well I've taken all these flavors and put them into a tart crust bound with my basic tart mix. One of the most exciting tastes in this dish is the eggplant. They eat almost like homemade eggplant chips!

SERVES 6

3 tablespoons olive oil
2 tablespoons unsalted butter
2 onions, sliced
1 garlic clove, crushed
Salt and freshly ground black pepper
1 large red bell pepper, seeded and
    thinly sliced
1 large green bell pepper, seeded and
    thinly sliced
1 recipe Basic Tart Mix (see p.120)

2 zucchini
6 (4 inch) (10 cm) or 1 (10 inch)
    (25 cm) Puff Pastry crusts, blind
    baked (see p.212)
1 large eggplant
1 cup all-purpose flour
1 teaspoon cayenne pepper
Oil for deep-frying
1 recipe Tomato Dressing (see p.233)

Pre-heat the oven to 400°F (200°C).

Heat a large pan and add 1 tablespoon of oil and the butter. When the butter starts to bubble, add the onions and crushed garlic, season with salt and pepper and cook for a few minutes until softened. Remove the onions from the pan and add a dash more olive oil to the pan. Allow the oil to heat, then fry the peppers, seasoned, until lightly colored. Return the onions to the pan, add the basic tart mix and thicken on the stove for about 15-20 minutes over a low heat. Do not allow to boil.

Split the zucchini lengthwise and cut into thin slices. Quickly shallow fry in a little oil in a hot pan until golden; about 1-2 minutes. These can now be added to the mix.

Spoon the mixture into the pastry crusts and finish in the pre-heated oven for 15-20 minutes for individual tarts or 30-35 minutes for one tart. The tart should only be set to the touch. If the mix has been chilled, it will take a further 8-10 minutes to cook.

Split the eggplant lengthwise, then cut across into thin slices. Mix together the flour and cayenne pepper with a pinch of salt. Dust the eggplant, then fry in hot deep oil until golden and crispy.

Place the tart in the center of a serving plate and spoon some tomato dressing around. Sit the eggplant chips on top of the tart and serve.

Stuffed Mushrooms

Stuffed mushrooms can be made so many different ways, with a range of fillings, toppings and textures. They work very well as vegetarian starters or main courses, or you can use prawns, mussels, bacon or other fish or meat ingredients. Rather than give you a basic recipe, I thought I would just share a few ideas.

I like to use Portobello mushrooms which have a good meaty texture and taste. It's best to half-cook them before adding any filling. They can then be stuffed, topped and baked. I always half-cook the mushrooms on a seasoned and buttered baking sheet under the broiler with a trickle of olive oil.

My favorite filling is cooked spinach. You can flavor this with garlic, leeks or even crispy smoked bacon pieces, then top the spinach with either a herb crust (see p.121) or thick slices of grated Cheddar or Gruyère. Bake the mushrooms in a pre-heated oven at 400°F (200°C), then finish under the broiler. These eat very well as a starter.

Other good fillings are a small, diced ratatouille finished with Parmesan or Stilton and spinach or just Stilton and breadcrumbs, leeks with mustard and Cheddar, or sliced tomatoes topped with Welsh rarebit mix.

Turn to p.130 to see how good they look.

Vegetarian Stir-fry

This really is tasty to eat as a starter or main course. It also works well with some other fish or meat dishes.

Serves 4

2 onions, sliced
2 tablespoons olive oil
4 tablespoons butter
8 oz (225 g) bean sprouts, blanched in
    boiling water
4 cups sliced mushrooms
1 lb (450 g) spinach, washed and torn

2 cups cooked thin spaghetti/noodles
1-2 tablespoons clear honey
2 tablespoons Spicy Marinade (see
    p.100)
Juice of 1 lime
Salt and freshly ground black pepper
6 green onions, diagonally sliced

The first thing is to start to cook the onions in a wok with the oil and butter for a couple of minutes. Add the blanched bean sprouts and sliced mushrooms and continue to cook over a moderate heat for 2 minutes. Add the spinach and cook for a few minutes until just wilted. Add the cooked spaghetti or noodles and cook for a further 2 minutes. Add the honey, spicy marinade and lime juice. Check for seasoning with salt and pepper, divide between four bowls and spoon over the liquid. Finish with the chopped green onions.

ABOVE *Making the Vegetarian Stir-fry (see p.129).*

OPPOSITE *In the foreground are mushrooms stuffed with spinach with an herb crust and behind are mushrooms stuffed with ratatouille (see p.128).*

Vegetables

———————

Some of these recipes will tell you how to get the maximum flavor from a bowl of sliced carrots, peas or beans.

There's all sorts of potato dishes, including one of my favorites, Irish Champ – lovely mashed buttery potatoes with green onions. I've also included a shocking pink recipe, Beet and Mashed Potato Cake. It's not just the color that shocks, it's the flavor, too. The Beet Fritters are crispy and golden, the Green Onion Potato Cakes are full of textures, and as for the stir-fry – you won't believe how quick and easy it is.

Mashed Potatoes

I find Russet are one of the best varieties for making mashed potatoes – then all you need to add is a little care.

Serves 4-6

2 lb (900 g) potatoes, quartered
Salt and freshly ground white pepper
½ cup (8 tablespoons) unsalted butter

½ cup heavy whipping cream or milk
Freshly grated nutmeg

Boil the potatoes in salted water until tender, about 20-25 minutes depending on size. Drain off all the water and replace the lid. Shake the pan vigorously which will start to break the potatoes. Add the butter and cream or milk a little at a time, while mashing the potatoes. Season with salt, pepper and nutmeg. The potatoes will be light, fluffy, creamy.

Green Onion Potato Cakes

This is a basic recipe which can be developed to suit so many other dishes. I like to add diced, smoked bacon which goes well with the green onions, and I serve this with a broiled herring dish(see p.79). It's also good to keep this a vegetarian dish, so why not just add grated cheese and onion and serve with a good tomato salad.

Serves 4

2 tablespoons unsalted butter
1 large bunch of green onions, finely
   diced
1½ cups or ¼ recipe Mashed Potatoes
   (see p.133), made without cream or
   milk

2 tablespoons olive oil
2 egg yolks
Salt and freshly ground white pepper
3 tablespoons all-purpose flour

Melt half the butter and fry the green onions quickly. While the mashed potatoes are still warm, add the olive oil, egg yolks and green onions and season with salt and pepper. Fold in the flour. The mix can now be divided into four or six patties about ½–¾ inch (1-2 cm) thick and pan-fried in the remaining butter and a little extra olive oil. The patties will take about 3-4 minutes on either side.

It is always best to pan-fry the patties as soon as the mix is ready. This will prevent it from becoming soggy. Once cooked, the patties can be kept and chilled, then baked through in the oven when needed. However, to eat them at their best, eat as soon as cooked.

Fondant Potatoes

These are potatoes that traditionally are shaped into barrels and then braised in chicken stock until all the stock has reduced and been absorbed. The potato is then packed with flavor. Well, I'm not changing this recipe too much, except the potatoes don't need to be shaped, they are just peeled and halved (see p.107).

SERVES 4

2 large potatoes, peeled and halved lengthwise
2½ cups Chicken Stock (see p.222) or Vegetable Stock (see p.223)

Salt
2 tablespoons unsalted butter

Pre-heat the oven to 400°F (200°C).

Sit the potatoes in a small, buttered baking tray or ovenproof dish. Pour in the stock, filling just three-quarters up the sides of the potatoes. Brush the potatoes with butter and lightly season with salt. Bring the stock to the simmer on top of the stove, then transfer to the pre-heated oven for 30-40 minutes. During this time the potatoes will be absorbing the stock. If the stock becomes almost dry, simply check the potatoes with a knife; they may be ready. If not, just add a little more stock, about ¼ inch (5 mm), and continue to cook.

For the last 10 minutes of cooking time, brush the potatoes with butter to help give them a nice golden color. They can also be finished under a hot broiler.

Champ

"Champ" is a classic dish of mashed potatoes and green onions. I'm not quite sure if it comes from Scotland or Ireland. I first experienced it in Northern Ireland, but have read in several books that it was first made in Scotland. It's one of those recipes that everybody believes their way is the only way to make it. Well, I'm not going to say that this is the way; I'll sit on the fence and just give you another version of champ – a delicious one!

The dish can be eaten on its own or just as a potato dish with boiled ham or bacon. I normally serve it with a boiled bacon collar, just spooned over with its cooking liquid and served with English mustard powder that's been mixed with water.

⅔ cup milk
8 oz (225 g) green onions, sliced
2-3 cups or ½ recipe Mashed Potatoes
    (see p.133), made without cream or
    butter

Salt and freshly ground white pepper
A pinch of freshly grated nutmeg
    (optional)
½-¾ cup (8-12 tablespoons) unsalted
    butter

Bring the milk to the simmer with the green onions. Add this to the mashed potatoes and season with salt and pepper. I like to add a pinch of nutmeg. Add half the butter to give a creamier texture. Spoon the potatoes into a bowl and make a well in the middle. The remaining butter can now be sat in the center. The champ is ready.

Variations

You can substitute chives, onions or even peas for the green onions. You can also make red champ with pieces of cooked beet added to the potatoes.

Champ.

Celeriac and Potato Dauphinoise

This is a French potato dish that has undergone one or two changes. The flavors are lovely and this eats well with most of the main courses.

SERVES 4

2 large onions, sliced
4 tablespoons unsalted butter
2½ cups heavy whipping cream
1 garlic clove, crushed

Salt and freshly ground black pepper
1 lb (450 g) potatoes, thinly sliced
1 large celeriac, peeled and thinly sliced

Pre-heat the oven to 350°F (180°C).

Cook the onions in half of the butter for 2-3 minutes without coloring, then allow to cool. Bring the cream to the boil with the crushed garlic and remaining butter and season with salt and pepper. Arrange the onions, potatoes and celeriac in a large ovenproof dish, making sure the potatoes are on the top and bottom. Overlap the top layer of potatoes to give a neater finish. Pour over the cream, making sure the potatoes are covered. Bake in the pre-heated oven for 45-60 minutes until the vegetables are tender and have absorbed the cream. Test the vegetables by piercing with a knife. Cover with foil if the potatoes are browning too quickly. Once cooked, finish, if necessary, under a hot broiler for that golden color.

Variations

For a creamier texture, sit the dish in a roasting pan filled with hot water to come three-quarters of the way up the dish, cover with foil and bake in the oven for 1-1¼ hours, finishing under the broiler.

This dish eats well without the celeriac as a straightforward Dauphinoise Potato. I also like to have anchovy fillets running through the center of the potatoes to add another taste.

Boulangère Potatoes

This is another potato dish with the potatoes simply sliced with onions and cooked in the oven in stock. It is a classic French recipe that is served in restaurants all over Britain, traditionally with roast rack or leg of lamb.

SERVES 4

2-4 tablespoons unsalted butter
2 onions, sliced
1½ lb (675 g) potatoes, thinly sliced
Salt and freshly ground white pepper

2 cups Chicken Stock (see p.222) or
Vegetable Stock (see p.223), warm

Pre-heat the oven to 450°F (230°C).

Melt a little of the butter and fry the onions until softened. Reserve some good round potato slices to arrange on the top of the dish, then mix the remainder with the cooked onions and season with salt and pepper. Place the mixture in a baking dish and cover with the reserved potato slices, overlapping them across the top. Pour over the warm stock and dot with the remaining butter. Cook in the pre-heated oven for 20 minutes until the potatoes begin to color. Reduce the oven temperature to 400°F (200°C) and cook for a further 40-50 minutes, pressing down the potatoes with a spatula occasionally for more even cooking. By the end of cooking, the potatoes will have absorbed the stock and should be golden and crispy on top. To finish, just sit the potatoes under the broiler to achieve that extra golden color.

Variations

There are a good many variations you can try. Add some strips of smoked bacon; sliced leeks; truffles (very nice – expensive, too!); sliced celeriac; sage and thyme – or just use your imagination!

Beet Fritters

These fritters eat very well with a classic accompaniment of just salt and vinegar, and also eat well if just dipped in sour cream or yogurt and chives. They make a good alternative vegetable dish or can be used as a vegetarian starter (using the right beer).

To cook beets, plunge them into boiling salted water, then return to the boil. The cooking time depends on age and size. Don't test them with a fork or they will bleed. Lift one out of the water after 30 minutes and try to pull back the skin with your thumb. If the skin comes off easily, the beet is cooked. If not, continue to test every 5–10 minutes. Once cooked, drain and leave to cool, then peel, cut in half and cut into ¾ inch (2 cm) wedges. You can serve them as they are with some salad dressing or vinegar, sugar and a little water mixed together and poured over, or you can try this!

SERVES 4

3½ cups self-rising flour	Oil for deep-frying
Salt	12 beet wedges
1¼ cups lager-style beer	Salt and freshly ground black pepper
	Malt vinegar (optional)

Mix the flour and salt into the lager until you have a smooth, thick batter with almost a glue-like consistency. Pre-heat a deep frying pan to 350°F (180°C). Season the beet wedges and dust with flour. Coat with batter. Drop into the hot fat and fry for a few minutes until crisp and golden. Remove and salt lightly. Sprinkle with vinegar before serving, if liked.

Variations

Parsnips also work well in this recipe. Peel and quarter the parsnips lengthwise, cut the root from the center and blanch the parsnips in boiling salted water for 2-3 minutes. Drain, cool and pat dry. Lightly flour, coat with batter and cook in the same way, then salt lightly before serving.

Beet Fritters.

Beet and Mashed Potato Cake

This dish goes well with venison, pheasant, pigeon or just about any game. It also eats well with most meats, making a roast leg of pork or lamb, for example, just that bit more interesting. Top it with spinach and a crumble mix to make a complete vegetarian dish.

SERVES 4

2 large onions, sliced
4 tablespoons unsalted butter
8 oz (225 g) beets, cooked and grated
¾ cup Mashed Potatoes (see p.133), made without milk or cream

Salt and freshly ground white pepper
1 tablespoon all-purpose flour

Cook the onion in half the butter for a few minutes until softened but not colored. Leave to cool.

Mix the beets with the potatoes, add the onions and season with salt and pepper. Stir well. The mix will be a shocking pink color. It can now be fried as one large cake or shaped into small cakes. Pre-heat a frying pan. Dust the cakes with a little flour and fry in the remaining butter over a medium heat for about 4-5 minutes until golden brown on each side.

Variations

This can become a sausage and beet cake by dicing and frying some sausage and bacon and adding it to the mix before frying it. Serve it with a fried egg on top and broiled tomatoes.

Try making potato and onion cake, top it with slices of corned beef, then thick slices of tomato, season and dot with butter then pop under the broiler. If you're feeling really mad, top the lot with slices of Cheddar and let it melt over the cake!

Glazed Carrots

Cooking carrots has become a very standard job. While they are a useful everyday vegetable, they are great to flavor so many things and I like cooking them this way to make them really tasty and exciting to eat.

SERVES 4

1 lb (450 g) carrots
A pinch of salt
Water

1 teaspoon sugar
2-4 tablespoons unsalted butter

The carrots can just be sliced into rings for this recipe, but I like to split them lengthwise, twice if they are thick, then cut them at an angle into ½ inch (1 cm) pieces. This gives more substance and texture to the vegetable. Place the carrots in a pan with a pinch of salt. Literally just cover, and only just, with water. Add the sugar and butter. Bring the water to the boil, then simmer until the carrots are just tender but still with a slight bite. The cooking time will be determined by how you have sliced them; 8-15 minutes.

Drain the liquid into another pan and boil to reduce until 5-6 tablespoons are left. In the reduction process, the butter and sugar content will thicken the liquid, giving you a glaze. Add a little more butter if you want to thicken it a little more. Add the carrots to the pan and re-heat in the glaze. This will give them a wonderful, appetizing shine. Check the seasoning and serve.

Green Beans and Runner Beans

Green beans must be the most popular vegetable in restaurants; what we consider a first-class vegetable. They need minimum preparation – just top and tail them – and cook quickly. You can even buy them ready trimmed in most supermarkets! Another advantage is that you can cook them hours in advance, refresh them in iced water, then re-heat them later when you are ready to eat.

The secret to keeping good color on any green vegetable is to make sure the water is salted and boiling rapidly before you add the vegetables, don't use a lid, and don't cook too many at once. For home cooking, it's best to cook only 1 lb (450 g) at a time. This is plenty for four to six portions.

To cook beans or any green vegetables, have a large pan three-quarters full of boiling water with a good pinch of salt. Drop in the beans and return the water to the boil. If the beans are extra fine they will be just about cooked; if just fine, cook for 30-45 seconds once the water has re-boiled. Check the beans during cooking; they should always have a good bite in them. Drain the beans and toss them in a tablespoon of butter, seasoning with salt and a good twist of pepper.

The exception to this method is spinach, which is best cooked from raw in melted butter. It will cook and create all its own juices.

Runner beans are another favorite. To prepare these, just top and tail them, pulling away the sinewy string on either side. Cut the beans at an angle into thin 2-3 inch (5-7.5 cm) strips. This way, the beans are cooked as soon as the water returns to the boil. If you prefer large pieces, cut them into 1 inch (2.5 cm) diamonds; these will take 1-2 minutes.

When cut into strips, runner beans leave lots of room for extra tastes. I like to mix them with sliced onions cooked until golden in butter with strips of smoked bacon.

*A selection of fresh runner beans,
green beans and carrots.*

Fresh Peas

Fresh peas are lovely to eat, providing they are properly cooked. Remember, don't try to cook too many at once, and don't cover the pan.

Once the peas have been shelled, bring a large pan of salted water to the boil. Drop in the peas, return the water to the boil and boil for 15–20 minutes, keeping the water boiling all the time. If the peas are not tender by that time, just keep boiling until they are ready. Drain off the peas, toss in butter and season with salt and pepper. Peas also eat well mixed with Glazed Carrots (see p.141); this then becomes a Flemish-style dish. Of course, you could substitute frozen peas.

This is a classic French dish called petits pois à la française. *It is almost braised peas with onions and lettuce, with the liquid thickened with a little flour. Well, I've changed it slightly and this is what I do.*

SERVES 4

4 tablespoons unsalted butter
2 onions, sliced
4 slices smoked bacon, cut into strips

¼–⅓ cup Chicken Stock (see p.222) or
　　Vegetable Stock (see p.223)
Salt and freshly ground black pepper
1 lb (450 g) peas, cooked

Melt 2 tablespoons of butter and cook the onions and bacon until slightly softened. Add the stock and bring to the boil. Add the remaining butter and season with salt and pepper. Quickly re-heat the peas for 30 seconds in a pan of boiling water, then drain off. Toss the peas in the reduced bacon and onion liquid and serve.

Fried Spinach, Mushrooms and Bean Sprouts

This eats well on its own but is even better with the Seared Spicy Pork Belly (see p.100).

SERVES 4

1½–2 lb (750–900 g) spinach
1–2 tablespoons olive oil
2 tablespoons unsalted butter
4 cups sliced mushrooms

8 oz (225 g) bean sprouts, blanched in
　　hot water
Salt and freshly ground black pepper
Juice of 1 lime

First remove the stalks from the spinach and tear the leaves carefully into small pieces. Wash the leaves and leave to dry.

Heat a wok or frying pan and add the olive oil and butter. Add the mushrooms and toss for 30 seconds. Add the bean sprouts and continue to cook for 2 minutes. Add the spinach and continue to stir for 1 minute. Add the seasoning and lime juice and cook for about 30 seconds more until the vegetables are just tender.

Braised Lentils

Braised lentils can be used in so many dishes – fish or meat – and are perfect as an accompaniment to a main course or as a vegetable dish in their own right.

SERVES 4

4 tablespoons unsalted butter
1 carrot, finely diced
1 small onion, finely diced
2 celery stalks, finely diced
1¼ cups (8 oz) (225 g) lentils

1 slice of bacon (optional)
3¾ cups Vegetable Stock (see p.223) or Chicken Stock (see p.222)
Salt and freshly ground black pepper

Pre-heat the oven to 400°F (200°C).

Melt the butter in an ovenproof casserole and fry the finely diced vegetables for a few minutes. Add the lentils and bacon, if using, and fry for a further minute. Add about 2½ cups of the stock, making sure the lentils are just covered with stock, and bring to a simmer. Cover with a lid and cook in the pre-heated oven for 30-40 minutes, stirring occasionally, until the lentils are tender. As the lentils cook, they will tenderize as they absorb the stock. You may need to add a little more stock during cooking.

You can serve the lentils straightaway, or they can be cooled and chilled. They will keep in the refrigerator for two to three days and can be re-heated in a spoonful of stock or water with a tablespoon of butter.

Variation

This recipe can also be made into lentil soup by doubling the quantity of stock. Bacon is a good flavoring for lentils, so try adding a small dice or piece of bacon during cooking. If you've had a boiled bacon collar or pork shoulder dish for lunch or dinner one day, then make sure that you keep all the stock it cooked in and dice any left-over bacon. With some chopped vegetables, you'll have an almost instant lentil and bacon soup to put together.

Desserts

When was the last time you indulged in a really good ice cream sundae? Well, if you think there's nothing new you can do with ice cream, turn to my Chocolate and Toffee Ice Cream Sundae on page 201. And don't stop there: I've dedicated my book to re-inventing the classic favorites with new flavors and textures. So don't miss any of my "adult-pleasing" creams, cookies and tarts — they're awesome!

ABOVE *Summer Fruit Ice Cream Sundae*
(see p. 204).
LEFT *Adding honey to Griddled Honey Apples (see p. 166).*

Pineapple Fritters

I like to serve these fritters with Coconut Ice Cream (see p.195) and Rum Custard Sauce (see p.215). It's almost like eating a hot Piña Colada cocktail! The fritters also eat well with whipped cream and Chocolate Sauce (see p.216).

Serves 4

1 small, ripe pineapple
1¼ cups sweet hard cider
1 cup all-purpose flour plus a little extra
    for coating

2 tablespoons sugar
Vegetable oil for deep-frying

Cut the outside skin from the pineapple, then split it into quarters. Remove the central core from all four pieces. Each quarter can now be cut into three leaving you with twelve large chunks.

To make the batter, mix together the cider, flour and sugar. Heat the oil to about 350°F (180°C). Lightly flour the pineapple chunks, then dip them into the batter and deep-fry for about 5 minutes until crispy and golden. You may need to do this in batches.

Pineapple and Almond Tart

This tart eats really well sitting on a rich Chocolate Sauce (see p.216) and topped with Coconut Ice Cream (see p.195). All those flavors work so well with pineapple. The pineapple should be fresh and ripe. This will be a deep yellow color with a moist sweet taste. If you find the pineapple to be firm and opaque in color, the fruit will need to be poached in some Stock Syrup (see p.217) until tender. This dish can also be made using a good quality canned pineapple. You can make this tart with lots of different fruits from apple and blackberry to raspberry, pear or peach. All these fruits work with different ice creams and sauces.

SERVES 6-8

About ⅔ recipe Shortcrust Pastry (see p.211)
½ fresh pineapple, peeled

2 tablespoons pineapple jam (optional)
1 recipe Almond Paste (see p.213)
Confectioners' sugar, sifted

Pre-heat the oven to 375°F (190°C) and grease a 10 inch (25 cm) tart pan.

Roll out the pastry, line the tart pan and leave to rest in the refrigerator. Cut the pineapple into ¾ inch (2 cm) cubes. For extra pineapple taste, spread some pineapple jam onto the pastry crust first before spooning in the almond paste and smoothing over.

Push the pineapple cubes into the almond paste. During the cooking of this tart the almond paste will become liquid and flood the tart pan. As the paste cooks it will develop a moist sponge cake texture. Bake the tart in the pre-heated oven. The tart will take between 45-60 minutes. The almond paste will rise slightly.

To give an extra finish and glaze to the tart, sprinkle liberally with confectioners' sugar and glaze under the broiler.

Note

For a different finish to the dish, liberally scatter diced fresh pineapple over the top of the tart 10 minutes before it is completely cooked and return it to the oven. The tart can still be finished with the confectioners' sugar glazed under the broiler, giving a slight burnt tinge to the pineapple.

Apricot and Almond Tart

For this recipe I'm using a large 11 inch (28 cm) diameter and 1½ inch (4 cm) deep tart pan which really does make a large dessert. The recipe can easily be cut down by half and a smaller 7 inch (18 cm) tart pan can be used. You can use whichever stock syrup you prefer for this recipe.

The tart eats well hot or cold and goes well with whipped cream, custard or ice cream and is great served with Christmas Pudding Ice Cream (see p.194).

SERVES 6-8

24 dried, pitted apricots
1¼ cups Stock Syrup (see p.217)
About ⅔ recipe Shortcrust Pastry (see p.211)

4 tablespoons apricot jam
1 recipe Almond Paste (see p.213)
Confectioners' sugar, sifted

Pre-heat the oven to 375°F (190°C). Butter and lightly flour a 11 inch (28 cm) tart pan.

Split the apricots through the middle, leaving circular discs of fruit. Warm the stock syrup with the fruits and then leave to cool. These can be prepared and chilled days in advance or left until the last minute and drained off before using. The stock will still keep in the refrigerator. This process softens the apricots even more and leaves them tender.

Roll out the pastry and use to line the tart pan. Heat the jam and reduce by half. Spread the jam over the pastry crust, then place 20 apricot pieces evenly over the jam. Spoon over the almond paste, leaving a smooth finish on top, and filling to about three-quarters of the way up to allow for it to rise during cooking. Bake in the pre-heated oven for 45 minutes. Remove from the oven and arrange the remaining apricots on top in a circular pattern. (If you put them on before cooking, they sink into the almond paste as it warms and loosens.) Return to the oven for a further 10-20 minutes until golden brown and just firming to the touch.

Sprinkle the tart liberally with confectioners' sugar and glaze under a hot broiler, allowing the sugar to caramelize and almost burn in places for a bitter sweet taste.

Apricot and Almond Tart.

Chocolate and Pear Brûlée

Chocolate and pears are a classic combination; the flavors work so well together. The texture of the brûlée has an almost chocolate-toffee consistency which can become more toffee-ish if you use extra chocolate.

I like to eat crème brûlées at room temperature so the consistency is similar to egg custard. However, this dessert can also be eaten chilled.

SERVES 4

8 egg yolks
¼ cup sugar
2½ cups heavy whipping cream
4 oz (100 g) or more good quality semi-
  sweet chocolate, grated

4-6 Poached Pear halves (see p.181) or
  canned pear halves
1 cup confectioners' sugar, sifted

Pre-heat the oven to 325°F (160°C).

Beat the egg yolks and sugar together in a bowl. Bring the cream to a boil and whisk it into the egg yolk mix. Sit the bowl over a pan of hot water and heat until the custard thickens, stirring all the time; it should have the consistency of heavy whipping cream. Add the grated chocolate and stir until melted. The mix should now be tasted. If the chocolate flavor is not strong enough, simply keep adding, stirring and tasting until you have the right flavor. Divide the chocolate custard between individual ½-⅔ cup ramekins and sit them in a roasting pan. Fill the pan with hot water to come three-quarters up the sides of the ramekins. Finish in the pre-heated oven for 20-30 minutes until the mix thickens and sets. Check the brûlées by removing a ramekin from the pan and shaking gently. The brûlée should be only slightly runny in the center. If the mix is still too liquid, return to the oven and check after a further 5 minutes. Once cooked, remove the ramekins from the oven and pan and allow to cool to room temperature.

To finish the dish, cut the pears lengthwise into slices and arrange overlapping on top of each dessert. Sprinkle liberally with confectioners' sugar and glaze under a hot broiler until you have a golden crisp sugar topping. To achieve a good glaze the confectioners' sugar may have to be applied two or three times.

Variations

It's also possible to slice a quarter of a pear per dessert, then dice the remaining fruit and place it in the bottom of the ramekins before adding the brûlée.

Steamed Sponge Cake

These desserts are real homey classics – just the sort of dessert to finish your meal, especially for a Sunday dinner. Steamed sponge cakes seem to be playing a big part in The Great British Revival. In fact, Steamed Lemon Sponge Cake was one of the, if not the, first dessert that I made. The sponge cake can be so light and fluffy to eat and will take on so many other flavors, many of which I am featuring here.

To make it a lot easier to turn out the desserts, use plastic molds which hold up very well to steaming, and when lightly pressed the cake should fall out easily. You can use ⅔ cup individual molds or a 4 cup mold.

SERVES 4-6

½ cup (8 tablespoons) unsalted butter
⅔ cup sugar
2 eggs
1 egg yolk

1½ cups self-rising flour
1-2 drops of milk, if needed
Lightly butter and flour 4 (⅔ cup) molds
    or 1 (3 cup) mold

Beat the butter and sugar together until almost white in color and the sugar has dissolved. This is easily achieved in an electric mixer. It does, however, take a little while to cream to this stage. Beat in one egg at a time, making sure after each egg is added that the mix is beaten until completely mixed and fluffy again. Once both eggs have been added, continue with the same process for the egg yolk. Most recipes will tell you now to fold in the flour slowly and carefully. Well, I want you to do quite the opposite. Add the flour and beat until all the flour has completely creamed into the mix but do not over-work. Add the milk if needed.

Spoon in the mixture, filling each mold three-quarters full. Cover the molds with lightly buttered squares of aluminum foil, just lightly folding the foil over the rims so the sponge cake can rise and push up the foil during cooking. Steam the cakes over boiling water, allowing 35-40 minutes for individual desserts or 1¼-1½ hours for the larger mold. Top up the boiling water as necessary during cooking.

Golden Syrup Sponge Cake

Golden syrup sponge cake is always a favorite - just add a generous spoon of syrup or light molasses to the cake batter and sit some more in the base of each mold and then steam. Pour a little more syrup or light molasses on top before serving (see overleaf).

Steamed Lemon Sponge Cake with Lemon Curd Ice Cream and Lemon Custard Sauce

This sponge cake eats beautifully with Lemon Curd Ice Cream and Lemon Custard Sauce (see preceding pages). If you feel this is all a bit too strong, simply serve the dessert with one or the other and some whipped cream.

SERVES 4-6

1 Steamed Sponge Cake recipe (see p.153)
Finely grated zest of 1 lemon
Juice of 1 lemon

A little milk
Lemon Curd Ice Cream (see p.197)
Lemon Custard Sauce (see p.215)

Add the lemon zest to the butter and sugar mixture in the basic sponge cake method, then continue to make the sponge cake until the flour has been added and mixed. Fold in the lemon juice and a little milk, if necessary. Because the zest was in at the beginning the flavor will become more powerful and strong. The cake can now be steamed in the usual way (see p.153).

PRECEDING PAGES *Clockwise, starting top left:*
Steamed Chocolate Sponge Cake (see p.160); Golden Syrup Sponge Cake (see p.153);
Steamed Lemon Sponge Cake with Lemon Curd Ice Cream
and Lemon Custard Sauce (see above);
Steamed Apricot Sponge Cake with Apricot Sauce (see p.159);
and Steamed Orange Sponge Cake with Hot Orange Sauce
and Marmalade Ice Cream (see p.158).

Steamed Lemon and Rhubarb Sponge Cake

Using the red currant jelly with the rhubarb is an optional extra that helps enrich the juices from the sugared rhubarb. If eaten cold, the mixture will almost set to jam. The beauty of the recipe is that so many other flavors work with it. A little ginger may be added, or you can use other fruits such as blackberries or blueberries. The rhubarb recipe can also be cooked a little more and then puréed and turned into a sorbet or ice cream (see p.189).

You can make individual cakes or one large one. The flavors of the rhubarb and lemon work really well together, and you can serve the dessert with whipping cream, Lemon Custard Sauce (see p.215) or even Vanilla Ice Cream (see p.190).

SERVES 4-6

1 lb (450 g) fresh rhubarb
2 tablespoons unsalted butter
1 cup sugar

1 tablespoon red currant jelly (optional)
1 Steamed Lemon Sponge Cake (see p.156)

Peel any coarse skin from the rhubarb stalks; young, tender rhubarb will not need to be peeled. Cut the rhubarb into ¾ inch (2 cm) pieces. Melt the butter in a pan until it begins to bubble. Add the rhubarb and stir gently for 1-2 minutes. Add the sugar and bring to the simmer. As the rhubarb is warming it will also be cooking. When it becomes tender, after about 4-5 minutes depending on size and ripeness, remove from the heat. Stir in the red currant jelly, if using. Allow the rhubarb mix to cool.

Butter and flour one large mold or individual molds. Spoon 4-5 tablespoons of the rhubarb into the large mold or 1 tablespoon into the individual molds, cover with the lemon sponge cake mix and finish and cook in the usual way (see p.153).

When the sponge cakes are cooked, re-heat the remaining rhubarb. Turn the cakes out onto serving plates and spoon some more fruit over the top.

Steamed Orange Sponge Cake with Hot Orange Sauce and Marmalade Ice Cream

This dessert gives us three different orange flavors from bitter to sweet, and also three different textures (see pp.154-55). It has to be my favorite steamed sponge cake. The whole dish is packed with orange flavor.

SERVES 4-6

½ cup (8 tablespoons) unsalted butter
⅔ cup sugar
2 eggs
1 egg yolk

Finely grated zest of 1 orange
1½ cups self-rising flour
Juice of 2-3 oranges, boiled to reduce by
    two-thirds, then cooled

For the Sauce

2½ cups fresh orange juice
2-4 tablespoons sugar
1 teaspoon arrowroot or cornstarch

1 tablespoon cold water
Marmalade Ice Cream to serve (see
    p.198)
A few fresh mint sprigs

To make the sponge cake, cream the butter and sugar together. Mix the eggs and egg yolk together and beat into the butter and sugar mix. Add the orange zest and fold in the flour. Add the orange juice, making sure it is cold.

Line six ⅔ cup molds or one 4 cup mold with butter and flour. Spoon in the sponge cake mix to fill three-quarters of the way up the mold and cover with buttered wax or parchment paper or aluminum foil. Steam individual cakes for about 35-40 minutes or one large cake for 1¼-1½ hours.

Meanwhile, make the orange sauce. Boil the orange juice until reduced by half, then add the sugar to taste (start with a tablespoon and add until you have the sweetness you want). Mix the arrowroot or cornstarch with the water, then whisk a few drops at a time into the simmering juice until you have a good sauce/coating consistency. Allow to cook for 3-4 minutes.

Once the sponge cake is cooked, just turn out and serve with a spoonful of marmalade ice cream, some hot orange sauce and a sprig of mint.

Variations

This is a recipe for a basic orange sauce. To change the flavor, some grated zest can be added or a little Cointreau, Grand Marnier or brandy can be added to lift the taste.

Steamed Apricot Sponge Cake with Apricot Sauce

This recipe has many alternatives – you can use dried or canned apricots, or even apricot jam. This, of course, makes it quite a rich dessert that is packed with flavor.

When buying dried apricots it's best to select "ready-to-eat" ones that still have about 25 percent moisture left in them, which leaves them soft enough to eat straight from the package. Also for this recipe choose the apricots which are still orange in color. The texture of this dish is lovely to eat. You have good soft apricots on top of a light fluffy sponge cake with the rich sauce. The best accompaniment is simply whipped cream or vanilla ice cream.

SERVES 4-6

12-16 dried apricots
1 15 oz (425 g) can halved apricots in
    syrup

1 Steamed Sponge Cake recipe (see
    p.153)
1 tablespoon apricot jam
Confectioners' sugar, sifted

It's best to start this recipe either in the morning or day before to achieve the best flavor from the apricots. To give them more moisture and flavor they should be soaked in some syrup, and with this recipe you don't even have to make it. Just open the canned apricots and pour off and keep the syrup. Warm the syrup and add the dried apricots. Leave them to stand for a few hours. The apricots should be a little softer and more juicy.

Grease and flour six ⅔ cup molds or one 4 cup mold.

You can now place three halves of apricot per portion, without syrup, into the bottom of the individual or large molds. If you have soaked some extra, then simply chop them up and mix into the basic sponge cake mix. Spoon the mix on top and steam as for the basic recipe (see p.153).

To make the apricot sauce, blend the canned apricots to a purée. Warm in a pan with the apricot jam, then add enough of the remaining syrup until you have a good sauce consistency. The sauce may taste a little sharp. To help this, just add some confectioners' sugar a pinch at a time until you have the right sweetness. Push the sauce through a sieve and it is ready.

Once the sponge cake is cooked, turn out onto a plate and spoon some of the warm sauce over.

Steamed Chocolate Sponge Cake

Along with steamed jam sponge cake, this has to be a children's favorite. In fact, I think it's a favorite for everyone (see pp.154–55). One of the pleasures of cooking is never allowing recipes to be over-strict. This dessert can have so many different textures and tastes added from walnuts and almonds to dates and orange zest – and many more.

There are two or three sauces which go very well with this dessert. Try Chocolate Sauce (see p.216), Coffee Custard Sauce (see p.215) or Pecan Nut Sauce (see p.168). It's all very rich but very tasty!

SERVES 4-6

1 recipe Steamed Sponge Cake (see p.153), omitting ½ cup of the self-rising flour

½ cup unsweetened cocoa powder
2-4 oz (50-100 g) good quality semi-sweet chocolate, grated

Simply follow the basic sponge cake recipe mixing the cocoa powder with remaining self-rising flour. Stir the grated chocolate into the mix to lift the flavor and texture.

To cook this dessert, only steam for 35 minutes if using individual molds or for 1½ hours in a large mold. This leaves it slightly softer in the center. Turn out and serve with the sauce of your choice. I also like to finish the dish with either grated chocolate or chocolate shavings.

Cloutie Dumpling

I ate this recipe for dessert when I visited Alan Craigie at the Creel Restaurant in the Orkneys while filming my television show. It was delicious. What did surprise me was that I had also eaten it that morning with my cooked breakfast! Now that's what I call variety.

Cloutie dumpling is a Scottish specialty. Cloutie comes from the word "clout" meaning cloth, which is what the dumpling is wrapped in before boiling. I would describe it as a light Christmas dumpling. For me, it ate best as a dessert with lots of whipped cream.

If you have any left over, just cut it into slices and shallow fry in butter for breakfast the next day.

SERVES 4-6

1⅓ cups self-rising flour
3 cups brown breadcrumbs
6 oz (175 g) shredded suet
¾ cup currants
1 cup raisins
1 cup golden raisins
1 teaspoon baking soda

A good pinch of ground ginger
A good pinch of freshly grated nutmeg
A good pinch of ground cinnamon
⅔ cup packed soft dark brown sugar
2 tablespoons light or dark molasses
1 cup milk

Simply mix all the ingedients together. Boil a large cloth then dust with flour. Place the mix in the cloth, then pull the cloth around, making a ball shape. Boil in a pan of water for 2-2½ hours, topping up as necessary, then unwrap, slice and serve with whipped cream.

Blackberry Jam Tart

I used to love jam tarts as a child: just sweet pastry tarts filled with jam. I thought they were really delicious. Well, this recipe is for a jam tart with a difference. I have always felt that a jam tart needed another texture, so read on and you'll see exactly what I mean!

For this recipe I'm going to use four individual tartlet pans, but an 11 inch (28 cm) tart pan will be fine. If you use a large tart pan, the pastry crust can be left raw before adding the almond mix, then all baked at the same time, in which case it will need 1–1¼ hours.

The jam tart eats well just with whipped cream. I also like to serve homemade Custard Sauce (see p.215) either cold or warm, or sometimes flavored with Calvados.

SERVES 4-6

6-8 oz (175-225 g) Puff Pastry (see p.212)	1½ cups ground almonds
¾ cup (12 tablespoons) unsalted butter	⅓ cup all-purpose flour
¾ cup sugar	3 eggs
	¾ cup Blackberry Jam (see p.210)

Pre-heat the oven to 350°F (180°C).

Roll out the pastry thinly and line the tart pans, leaving any excess pastry hanging over the edge. This will prevent the pastry from shrinking back into the mold during baking. Leave to rest for 20 minutes. Line the pastry with wax or parchment paper and fill with baking beans or rice and bake in the pre-heated oven for 15–20 minutes until the pastry is cooked and set. Remove the paper and beans and cut off any excess pastry hanging over the edges. To do this, simply take a sharp knife, position it at the top of the tart pan and cut all the pastry away. By cutting this way the pastry will be neatly flush with the tart pan.

You can, of course, make the filling in a food processor. Beat the butter and sugar together until well creamed. Fold in the almonds and flour. Beat in one egg at a time, making sure they are well mixed in. Spoon the almond filling into the pastry crust, leaving it about ¹⁄₁₆ inch (2 mm) from the top. (If you find you have some mix left over, then simply chill it and it will keep for up to one week.) Bake the tarts in the pre-heated oven, allowing 30-35 minutes for the small tarts or 45-60 minutes for a large tart. When cooked, the tarts will be firm to the touch and a knife inserted in the center will come out almost clean.

Once cooked the almond sponge cake mix should have risen slightly. This can simply be sliced off the top to expose the sponge cake. While the tart is still warm, spoon some of the jam over the tart until just covered. Return to the oven for 1–2 minutes by which time the jam will be making its way through the sponge cake. To serve, simply remove the tart pan sides and eat either hot or cold.

Variations

We all know what a great combination blackberry and apple is. If you really want to make this different and give other tastes then simply add some grated apple to the almond mix, or place poached apples or pears in the pastry crusts before spooning on the mix. This gives you different textures as well as tastes.

Treacle Tart

This is a very quick and easy recipe. It has, like so many other recipes, many alternatives. Half a teaspoon of ground ginger works very well, so does the addition of a little grated orange zest, or you can enrich the whole recipe with the addition of a few tablespoons of heavy whipping cream and one or two eggs. You can eat it on its own or with whipped cream or vanilla ice cream.

Serves 4

1 recipe Sweet Pastry (see p.211)
4 tablespoons unsalted butter
10 tablespoons light molasses

4 cups fresh breadcrumbs
Finely grated zest and juice of 1 lemon

Pre-heat the oven to 400°F (200°C).

Roll out the pastry and use to line a 9 inch (23 cm) tart pan. Cover with wax or parchment paper and baking beans or rice and bake in the pre-heated oven for 10–15 minutes until set. Remove the paper and beans. Reduce the oven temperature to 350°F (180°C).

Melt the butter and molasses together. Add the breadcrumbs and lemon juice and zest. Pour the mix into the pastry crust and bake in the oven for 20 minutes. If the treacle filling is bubbling, then remove from the oven. If it is not quite at that stage, cook for a further 5–10 minutes. When the treacle is at the bubbling/sizzling stage, remove the tart from the oven and allow to settle. The tart can be eaten warm or cold.

Gypsy Tart

This is a recipe I had been searching for for years. It's a dessert I remember from school days and it was my favorite. When I found somebody who knew the dish and was given the recipe I couldn't believe how simple it is – and it still tastes great.

SERVES 6

About ⅔ recipe Shortcrust Pastry (see p.211)

1 (14 oz) (400 g) can evaporated milk
2¼ cups dark brown sugar

Pre-heat the oven to 400°F (200°C).

Roll out the pastry and use to line a 10 inch (25 cm) tart pan. Line with wax or parchment paper and baking beans and bake in the pre-heated oven for 15-20 minutes until cooked. Leave to cool.

Whisk the evaporated milk and sugar together for 10-15 minutes until light and fluffy. The mix should be coffee colored. Pour the mix into the pastry crust and bake in the oven for 10 minutes. The gypsy tart will now have a slightly sticky surface but will not set completely until it has been left to cool. Serve cold. I told you this recipe was easy!

Toffee

This really is amazing. When I show people the results, most just can't believe it. As you can see you don't need a lot of ingredients! The toffee is great for so many things: crumbles, creams, ice creams and sauces. You'll find some of the recipes in the book.

MAKES 14 oz (400 g)

1 (14 oz) (400 g) can sweetened condensed milk

All you have to do is place the can of condensed milk (totally unopened) into a pan and cover with cold water, making sure the can is completely covered. Bring to the boil and continue to simmer for 3 hours (no less!). Top up with boiling water as necessary and make sure you don't let the pan boil dry. Leave to cool down in the pan. The toffee is now made and can be kept chilled in the unopened can until the date runs out.

Toffee Cream

The standard proportions for this recipe are one can of Toffee to 2 cups of cream, but this makes a lot of cream, so it is best to make it in a smaller quantity.

SERVES 4

½ (14 oz) can Toffee (see p.164)   1 cup heavy or regular whipping cream

Stir the toffee in a bowl to loosen. If you're looking for a thick pouring cream, then simply add all the cream and whisk in until well mixed (regular whipping cream works well for this). If you want a thick and light cream, then use heavy whipping cream, just adding a quarter of the cream and whisking until thickened, then adding another quarter, and so on until everything is mixed. The toffee cream may still seem to be a little soft, so it's best to make this 1–2 hours before you need it and then chill it in the refrigerator. This will give the cream a totally new texture and, when spooned onto the plate, it will hold its shape.

Griddled Honey Apples with Toffee Cream

This must be the easiest and quickest apple dessert there is, so if you're ever stuck and time is running out, have a go! It's great to eat with the Toffee Cream but also works really well with just whipped cream or Vanilla Ice Cream (see p.190).

To speed up the glazing of the top, I use a gas gun, which works really well to caramelize sugar. However, please don't use one of these unless you're very familiar with them.

SERVES 2

3 apples, peeled and cored
1 tablespoon unsalted butter
4 teaspoons clear honey

2-3 tablespoons confectioners' sugar, sifted
Toffee Cream (see p.165) to serve
2 sprigs fresh mint (optional)

Slice the apples across through the middle to give six thick apple rings in total. Warm a frying pan and add the butter. Sit the apples middle-side-down into the pan and fry until the apples become a rich brown with tinges of burnt around the edges to give a bittersweet apple taste. Turn the apples and continue to cook over a medium heat for 1-2 minutes (or you can place them in a medium oven for 1-2 minutes until the apples become just tender).

Spoon the honey on top of the apples. Spoon the confectioners' sugar into a sifter and sprinkle well over the top. Finish under a hot broiler until the sugar becomes crispy. To increase the crunchy topping, just sprinkle more confectioners' sugar on top and re-glaze.

To serve the apples, sit three pieces onto each plate and serve with thick toffee cream and a sprig of mint.

Griddled Honey Apples with Toffee Cream.

Chocolate Fudge Cake with Pecan Nut Sauce

This cake is rich, sticky and very tasty. You won't be able to eat it too often but every now and again it's a wonderful treat. This makes quite a large cake but it is worth the effort. It keeps brilliantly for days in the refrigerator and can be simply microwaved a portion at a time or as a whole cake. To serve the cake just pour the pecan sauce over each slice.

SERVES 8

6 eggs
1⅔ cups sugar
A few drops vanilla extract
8 oz (225 g) good quality semi-sweet
     chocolate

1 cup (16 tablespoons) unsalted butter
1 cup ground almonds
2½ cups fresh white breadcrumbs

For the Pecan Nut Sauce

1 cup packed soft brown sugar
½ cup (8 tablespoons) unsalted butter

⅓ cup heavy whipping cream
¼–½ cup chopped pecan nuts

Pre-heat the oven to 350°F (180°C) and grease an 8 × 10 inch (20 × 25 cm) baking sheet. The baking sheet needs to be at least 1 inch (2.5 cm) deep to achieve the right texture.

Whisk together the eggs, sugar and vanilla extract until the mixture forms stiff peaks. Melt the chocolate with the butter in a bowl over warm water. Pour onto the egg and sugar mixture and then fold in the ground almonds and breadcrumbs. The mix will be very loose, almost liquid. Pour the mix into the prepared baking sheet and bake in the pre-heated oven for 50-60 minutes. The texture of the cake should be cooked but almost stodgy and moist. The cake should be left to rest for 10 minutes before serving.

To make the sauce, place the sugar, butter and cream in a saucepan and bring to the boil. Simmer the sauce until the sugar has dissolved. Stir in the pecan nuts. The sauce is now ready.

Chocolate Mousse

This is a rich and light chocolate mousse which can be served in glasses or molds. It can also be layered between Steamed Chocolate Sponge Cake (see p.160) in a terrine mold or round cake pan.

SERVES 8

5 oz (150 g) good quality semi-sweet chocolate
1¼ cups unsalted butter, diced
1¼ cups unsweetened cocoa powder

1¼ cups heavy whipping cream
1 cup sugar
6 eggs, separated

Chop the chocolate and melt it slowly in a bowl over a pan of hot water. Add the butter and let it melt in the warmth of the chocolate. Add the cocoa powder and whisk in until the mix is smooth. Whisk the cream until it forms soft peaks, then reserve in the refrigerator. Whisk half the sugar with all the yolks until pale and fluffy. Whisk the remaining sugar and egg whites together until they form stiff peaks.

Fold the chocolate mix with the egg yolks and sugar, add the meringue mix and lastly fold in the cream. The mousse can now be set in glasses or molds and needs half a day minimum to set.

Variations

If you wish to make this into a chocolate mousse cake or terrine, simply cut the sponge cake to fit the mold, layer it with the mousse and set in the refrigerator. The sponge cake can now be finished with the chocolate coating recipe on page 172 to make a really spectacular cake.

Irish Chocolate Coffee Cake

This recipe was given to me by a close friend, Gabrielle, who produces my television show. We often have different ideas about cooking and filming, but one thing is for sure, we both want the same results, and with this dish she won. It eats and keeps beautifully, especially when flavored with good Irish whisky!

MAKES 1 (8 inch) (20 cm) cake

6 oz (175 g) good quality semi-sweet chocolate

4-6 tablespoons strong black coffee

2-4 tablespoons Irish whisky

⅓ cup sugar

½ cup (8 tablespoons) unsalted butter at room temperature

3 eggs, separated

A pinch of salt

½ cup ground almonds

A few drops of almond extract

½ cup all-purpose flour, sifted

For the Icing

4 oz (100 g) good quality semi-sweet chocolate

2 tablespoons whisky or strong coffee

½ cup (8 tablespoons) unsalted butter

Pre-heat the oven to 350°F (180°C). Butter and flour an 8 inch (20 cm) cake pan.

Melt the chocolate, coffee and whisky in a bowl over a pan of simmering water, then cool to room temperature. Reserve a tablespoon of sugar, then cream together the remaining sugar with the butter until you have a pale yellow, fluffy mixture. Beat in the egg yolks until well blended. Whisk the egg whites and salt until soft peaks form. Sprinkle on the tablespoon of sugar and beat until stiff peaks form. With a rubber spatula, blend the melted chocolate into the butter and sugar mixture, then stir in the ground almonds and extract.

Fold in a quarter of the egg whites, sift in a quarter of the flour, then continue folding and sifting alternately until everything is blended. Turn the mixture into the prepared cake pan, pushing the mixture up to the rim with the spatula. Bake in the middle of the pre-heated oven for about 25–30 minutes. The cake is done when it has puffed, and a skewer pushed into the middle comes out clean. Allow the cake to cool. It must be thoroughly cold to be iced.

To make the icing, melt the chocolate and whisky or coffee in a bowl over a pan of simmering water until you have a smooth cream. Remove the bowl from the heat and beat in the butter a tablespoon at a time. Stand the bowl over cold water and beat until the chocolate mixture is cool and of spreading consistency. Spread it over the cake and serve with Cheesecake Cream (see p.180).

Irish Chocolate Coffee Cake with Cheesecake Cream (see p. 180).

Chocolate Terrine

This is the sort of dessert for a special dinner party. It's rich in texture and taste and eats like a chocolate dream. One of the big advantages of making this dish is that it freezes so well and doesn't spoil. So if you've got a party coming up, make this now and just pop it in the freezer ready for the big day. The best size terrine mold to use is a Le Creuset 11½ × 3½ inches (29 × 9 cm). The terrine mold is lined with a chocolate sponge, filled with a chocolate mousse and then coated with more chocolate.

SERVES 12

For the Cake

1 cup sugar
5 eggs, separated

1 cup unsweetened cocoa powder

For the Mousse

6 oz (175 g) good quality semi-sweet
    chocolate
¾ cup (12 tablespoons) unsalted butter
¾ cup unsweetened cocoa powder

1¼ cups heavy whipping cream
4 eggs, separated
¾ cup sugar

For the Chocolate Coating

½ cup milk
⅓ cup heavy whipping cream

10 oz (275 g) good quality semi-sweet
    chocolate, chopped
5 tablespoons unsalted butter, chopped

Pre-heat the oven to 325°F (160°C) and butter and line a 16 × 12 inch (40 × 30 cm) baking sheet. Line a 11½ × 3½ inch (29 × 9 cm) terrine with wax or parchment paper or plastic wrap.

To make the cake, mix half the sugar with the egg yolks and whisk until pale and fluffy. Whisk the egg whites until they form soft peaks, then add the remaining sugar and continue to whisk to a stiff meringue. Fold the cocoa into the egg yolk mix, then whisk in a quarter of the meringue mix. Carefully and lightly fold in the remaining meringue. Spread the mix in the prepared pan. Bake in the pre-heated oven for about 20-30 minutes. Leave to cool.

To make the mousse, melt the chocolate with the butter in a bowl over a pan of warm water until it binds to a thick cream consistency. Add the cocoa and beat until completely smooth and cooled. Whisk the cream until it forms soft peaks, then chill. Whisk the egg yolks with half the sugar until white and fluffy. Fold into the chocolate mix. Whisk the egg whites with the remaining sugar to meringue stage, then fold into the chocolate mix. Now fold in the whipped cream.

Cut the cold cake into four, making sure you measure from the mold, then line the base and sides, saving one piece for the top. Pour the chocolate mousse into the mold, then place the remaining piece of sponge cake on top. Chill for for 2–3 hours or freeze.

The chocolate coating finishes and really lifts the dessert. Bring the milk and cream to the boil, then pour on to the chocolate and butter. Stir until melted and blended. Cool until thick and at room temperature. To cover the terrine, remove from the refrigerator or freezer, spoon some on top and spread on until completely covered. Return to the refrigerator or freezer until set.

To finish, turn out the terrine onto a small board or tray, then spoon over the remaining chocolate coating and spread evenly over the cake. The terrine will, of course, no longer fit in the mold and so can be kept chilled or frozen on the tray or board. Once the coating has completely set, just cover with plastic wrap.

The terrine will make at least 12 portions. However, the finished dish can be cut into 4 and then frozen so that it can be eaten whenever you like.

Variations

This dessert can be made a lot easier by simply sitting half the cake into an 8 inch (20cm) pastry ring lined with wax or parchment paper and then pouring the mousse on top and finishing with another layer of cake. This can then be set in a refrigerator or freezer. Remove the pastry ring and the lining and finish with the chocolate coating. It will look like a rich chocolate cake but is in fact a rich chocolate mousse.

This chocolate dessert eats very well with either Orange Custard Sauce (see p.215) or Coffee Custard Sauce (see p.215).

OVERLEAF *Clockwise, starting from the left:*
Basic Tuile Cookies (see p.176); Gingerbread Cookies (see p.179);
Brandy Snap Cookies (see p.176); Chocolate Brownies (see p.178);
and Shortbread Cookies (see p.177).

Basic Tuile Cookies

This is a very basic tuile cookie recipe (see preceding pages). They eat very well with ice creams and make good baskets to sit the ice cream in. This mix keeps for up to a week if kept chilled. You can also change the flavor by adding the finely grated zest of 1 lemon or 1 orange (or both) or a little dried coconut.

Serves 4

9 tablespoons unsalted butter	3 egg whites
1¼ cups confectioners' sugar, sifted	1 cup all-purpose flour

Soften the butter and add the confectioners' sugar, beating until white. Add the egg whites and fold in the flour. The mix is ready and should now be chilled to set.

Pre-heat the oven to 350°F (180°C) and butter a baking sheet.

Spread the mix very thinly into 5 inch (13 cm) discs. This can be made easy by cutting a 5 inch (13 cm) circle from a thin plastic ice cream tub lid, then just placing it on the tray and spreading the mix in, keeping level with the lid. Bake the tuiles in the pre-heated oven for 5-6 minutes until totally golden brown. Remove from the tray while still hot and place over a tin can or mold to shape the basket.

Variations

If you wish to serve these as cookies to go with your coffee or serve separately with ice creams, then simply make 2½ inch (6 cm) discs and bake them the same way. To shape them, take the center roll from plastic wrap or aluminum foil and cut it lengthwise to give two semi-circular halves. Sit the warm cookies into the mold to set.

Brandy Snap Cookies

Brandy snap cookies are easy to make and can be made into various shapes and sizes (see preceding pages). I like to serve them with sorbets and ice creams. If you roll this mix into balls the size of a 25 cent piece and push them onto a buttered tray, the mix will spread to give you a disc big enough to place over or in a cup or over a aluminum can to make a basket for your ice creams. But always make sure that you keep a good distance between each one on the tray or you'll have just one large tray of brandy snap!

MAKES about 24

½ cup (8 tablespoons) unsalted butter
½ cup sugar
¼ cup light molasses

1 cup all-purpose flour
A pinch of ground ginger
A pinch of ground cinnamon

Place the butter, sugar and molasses in a pan and heat gently to dissolve. Remove from heat. Mix the flour with the ginger and cinnamon, then beat into the sugar mixture. Leave to cool.

Pre-heat the oven to 350°F (180°C) and grease two baking sheets.

Roll the mixture into balls the size of a 25 cent piece and place well spaced out on the prepared trays. Bake in the pre-heated oven for 7-10 minutes until golden brown with a perforated texture. Leave to cool slightly for a minute before removing from the tray and molding over a tea cup or round the handle of a wooden spoon. If the snaps cool before you can finish shaping them all, just pop them back in the oven to warm slightly.

Shortbread Cookies

This recipe works best if piped onto a greased baking sheet.

MAKES about 16

1 cup (16 tablespoons) unsalted butter
⅓ cup sugar

3½ cups all-purpose flour
5 teaspoons cornstarch

Pre-heat the oven to 350°F (180°C) and grease and line a baking sheet.

Cream together the butter and sugar until the sugar has dissolved into the fat. Sift the flour and cornstarch together and fold into the butter mix. Pipe the mix onto the baking sheet and bake in the pre-heated oven for 20 minutes until golden brown. Leave to cool on a wire rack. The cookies eat very well when sprinkled with sugar.

Variations

Lightly roll the shortbread mix about ½-¾ inch (1-2 cm) thick and 8 inches (20 cm) in diameter and place it in a tart pan. Mark it into eight pieces and prick all over with a fork before cooking. It will take about 30-35 minutes. Turn to pp.174-75 for a photograph.

Chocolate Brownies

Here are two alternative chocolate brownie recipes (see pp.174–75). The first is very rich and tasty and can be used even as petits fours or just as a cookie to go with ice cream. Remember that when melting butter or chocolate, don't let it heat above room temperature.

SERVES 4

1⅓ cups sugar
4 eggs
1 cup (16 tablespoons) unsalted butter
¾ cup unsweetened cocoa powder
⅔ cup all-purpose flour

8 oz (225 g) good quality semi-sweet
    chocolate
1 cup chopped hazel or pecan nuts
4 oz (100 g) white chocolate, cut into
    ½ inch (1 cm) chunks

Pre-heat the oven to 350°F (180°C) and lightly grease an 8 inch (20 cm) pan.

Beat together the sugar and eggs, making sure the sugar has completely dissolved. Melt the butter and whisk into the eggs. Sift together the cocoa and flour and add to the butter and egg mix. Melt the chocolate in a bowl over a pan of warm water, then stir in. Add the chopped nuts and white chocolate. Turn the mix into the prepared pan and bake in the pre-heated oven for 30-40 minutes. Leave to cool, then cut into wedges or squares.

Quick Chocolate "Brownies"

This recipe is even simpler and quicker to make than the one above, and it also goes well with ice creams.

SERVES 4

14 tablespoons unsalted butter
¼ cup sugar
1 teaspoon vanilla extract
¼ cup chopped dates (Medjools are
    best)

1⅓ cups all-purpose flour
1 teaspoon baking powder
2 cups cornflakes, crushed
¼ cup unsweetened cocoa powder

Pre-heat the oven to 350°F (180°C) and grease an 8 inch (20 cm) pan.

Cream the butter and sugar together. Add all the other ingredients. Spoon the mixture into the prepared pan and bake in the pre-heated oven for 25-30 minutes.

Gingerbread Cookies

These cookies taste delicious if you add some chopped pecan nuts or dates – or both (see pp.174–75). If you are using dates or nuts, simply stir them in with the evaporated milk.

MAKES about 20

1¾ cups all-purpose flour
¼ teaspoon salt
2 teaspoons baking soda
1 heaped teaspoon ground ginger
½ teaspoon cinnamon

4 tablespoons unsalted butter
¾ cup packed light brown sugar
¼ cup light molasses
1 tablespoon evaporated milk

Pre-heat the oven to 350°F (180°C) and grease two baking sheets.

Sift together the flour, salt, soda and spices. Heat the butter, sugar and molasses until dissolved. Leave to cool. Once cooled, mix into the dry ingredients with the evaporated milk to make a dough. Chill for 30 minutes.

Roll out the cookie dough to about ¼ inch (5 mm) thick and cut into fingers, circles or even gingerbread men! Place on the baking sheets, allowing a little space to spread. Bake in the pre-heated oven for 10-15 minutes.

Keeping an eye on the kitchen.

Cheesecake Cream

I like to serve this cheesecake recipe just as a cream. Of course, it can be spread on to a graham cracker crust and covered with a fruit topping for a classic cheesecake. Using this recipe as a cream gives it many more options, from serving with summer fruits, poached fruits, chocolate cake (especially the one on p.170) or even ice cream and raspberry sauce. It also eats very well if flavored with honey and a drop of Irish whisky. The other bonus is that it's quick and easy to make. The following quantities can be halved to make less.

SERVES 6-8

¼ cup sugar
1 lb (450 g) soft cream cheese

2½ cups heavy whipping cream, lightly
   whipped

Beat the sugar into the cream cheese until the sugar has dissolved and creamed. Fold in the lightly whipped cream. It is important that the cream is only lightly whipped. This will prevent the cream from becoming over-beaten and separating when mixing with the cream cheese. Place the cheesecake in a suitable bowl or dish and set in the refrigerator for about an hour.

Once the cream has set, it can be served in the bowl or shaped between two spoons to serve on the plate.

Variations

Lots of other flavors can be added to this mix. One of my favorites is toffee. To make a toffee cream, simply add a can of toffee (see p.164) to the cream cheese mix before folding in the whipped cream.

To make a chocolate version, melt 4-8 oz (100-225 g) of good quality semi-sweet chocolate, only allowing the chocolate to reach room temperature. The cream cheese must also be at room temperature and not chilled as this would set the cream when added. Simply mix the chocolate with the cream cheese and sugar, then fold in the whipped cream and set in the refrigerator. The 4 oz (100g) is the minimum amount of chocolate; your taste will determine the rest, but the more chocolate you add, the firmer the cream will be.

Poached Pears

This is an easy recipe to follow using simple quantities of two parts water to one part sugar, for example, 2 cups of water to 1 cup of sugar. The best pears to use are Bosc which have a good sweet taste and texture (see overleaf).

The pears can be used for many dishes like the Chocolate and Pear Brûlée (see p.152). They can also be made into a French classic, Poire Belle Hélène, which is poached pear with Vanilla Ice Cream (see p.190) and Chocolate Sauce (see p.216). This dish eats and looks very good if served in a Tuile Cookie basket (see p.176). You could also use some poached pear in a sundae glass layered with Vanilla Ice Cream (see p.190), pecan nuts, Chocolate Sauce (see p.216) and finished with Toffee Cream (see p.165). Now that is a rich dessert!

Serves 6

6 pears (Bosc, Bartlett, Anjou)   4 cups water
½ lemon   2¼ cups sugar
1 vanilla bean or cinnamon stick
   (optional)

Peel the pears, then cut them in half. Remove the core and the vein of stalk running from the center to the top of the pear by cutting diagonally on either side of the vein. The pears can now be lightly rubbed with the lemon to prevent discoloration. Sit the pears in a pan with the lemon and vanilla or cinnamon, if using, and cover with the water and sugar. Cover with wax or parchment paper and bring to the boil. Simmer for a few minutes, then remove from the heat, leaving the pears to cool in the syrup.

The pears can now be kept chilled in the syrup with the lemon and vanilla or cinnamon in an airtight container until ready to be used.

ABOVE *Poached Pears (see p.181) and Poached Peaches (see p.184).*

OPPOSITE *Peach Melba (see p.185).*

Poached Peaches

Before poaching the peaches, they should be skinned. This is achieved by lightly scoring the peach skin all the way around the fruit with a sharp knife. Plunge the fruits into boiling water for a few seconds and then into cold water. This method is called blanching – very similar to skinning a tomato. The skin will now peel off.

These peaches eat very well as almost a dessert on their own or halved and used in a great Auguste Escoffier classic – Peach Melba (see preceding pages).

SERVES 4

4-8 peaches, skinned
½ lemon
½ cinnamon stick (optional)

1¼ cups water
1¼ cups white wine
1 cup sugar

Sit the skinned peaches in a pan with the lemon and cinnamon stick, if using. Pour the water and white wine on top and add the sugar. If you find this is not enough you can add either half or the same quantities again. Cover with some wax or parchment paper and bring to the boil. Simmer the peaches for 4–5 minutes (3–4 minutes if they are very ripe and soft), then leave to cool in the syrup. If you have any problems keeping the fruit submerged in the syrup, simply sit a plate on top to hold them in place. The peaches are now ready and can be used straightaway (even while still warm) or chilled. If you wish to keep them for some time then seal them in airtight jars.

Peach Melba

I like to serve Peach Melba in Tuile Cookie baskets (see p.176). It's simply Vanilla Ice Cream (see p. 190) topped with poached peaches and then finished with Melba Sauce. I also like to add whipped cream flavored with fresh vanilla and sprinkled with toasted almonds, but this isn't essential. The Melba Sauce can be spooned onto the plate and the finished basket placed on top (see p.182).

Melba Sauce

Melba sauce, of course, is the sauce that goes with Peach Melba. There are many ways of making this raspberry sauce. This particular recipe gives a good balance of fruitiness to sweetness, but if you want a really quick version then simply boil ¾ cup of raspberry jam with 5 tablespoons of water and then strain through a sieve; or mix 2 cups of fresh raspberries with 1 cup of confectioners' sugar, push through a sieve and add a squeeze of lemon juice. Well, there's two recipes. Now here's mine.

SERVES 4

2 cups frozen raspberries, thawed   ¾ cup raspberry jam
⅔ cup sugar

Heat the raspberries with ¼ cup of the sugar until dissolved, then bring to the simmer. Push through a sieve to make a raspberry purée. Mix the purée with the remaining sugar and the jam and bring to the boil. Simmer for 3-4 minutes, then strain through a sieve. The sauce is ready and can be eaten hot or cold with many desserts.

Iced Cranachan Parfait

This is a Scottish recipe which is traditionally served at Halloween with soft red berries. It can also be made into an ice cream by replacing the cream with Vanilla Ice Cream (see p.190), but this recipe is an iced terrine which eats well with a drizzle of honey, or with a raspberry sauce and fresh raspberries.

This recipe is for a 10 inch (25 cm) terrine mold, but you can halve the quantities and use four individual ½–⅔ cup size ramekins.

SERVES 4

1 cup sugar
8 egg yolks
2½ cups heavy whipping cream
4 teaspoons clear honey

2–2⅔ cups oatmeal, toasted
Whisky to taste (optional)
Clear honey to serve

Whisk the egg yolks and sugar until pale and the mixture trails off the whisk in thick ribbons. (This is easier if you place the bowl over a pan of warm water.) Pour on the cream and continue to whisk (cold) until the cream begins to thicken. Fold in the honey, toasted oatmeal and whisky to taste. Pour into the terrine or individual molds and freeze until firm.

The cranachan can now be sliced and served.

Iced Chocolate Parfait

Sweet parfaits are like freezing a sweet sabayon. They take on a light ice cream texture. The quantities here will fill a 10 inch (25 cm) terrine mold, or you can use individual ½–⅔ cup ramekins. The ingredients may look a little costly, but remember there are quite a lot of portions in a terrine – or you can simply make half the recipe. Serve the parfait as it is or with the rich Chocolate Sauce (see p.216), Orange Custard Sauce (see p.215) or Coffee Custard Sauce (see p.215). Of course, if you really want to finish this dessert with a little extra, then cover it with Chocolate Coating (see p.172). This gives the parfait a lovely finish and another texture.

SERVES 8

7 egg yolks	6 oz (175 g) good quality semi-sweet
½ cup sugar	chocolate
	2½ cups heavy whipping cream

Line a 10 inch (25 cm) terrine with plastic wrap.

Whisk the egg yolks and sugar in a bowl over warm water until thick and at least doubled in volume. Melt the chocolate in a bowl over a pan of hot water, then mix with the yolks and sugar. Pour on the heavy whipping cream and whisk until a soft peak is reached. The parfait is ready to freeze in the terrine or in individual molds.

Note

The heavy whipping cream can be whisked separately to soft peaks and then lightly folded with the chocolate mix.

Fresh Fruit Salad

Fresh fruit salad has endless combinations. It's basically prepared fruits all mixed together. The recipe here for fruit salad is just to give you an idea and a basic recipe to work from. Some fruits have a coarser texture and eat a lot better if just lightly softened in Stock Syrup (see p.217). Or you can try using Poached Peaches (see p.184) or Poached Pears (see p.181).

Any soft red fruits should always be added just before serving to prevent them coloring the other fruits.

One particular favorite of mine is summer fruit salad which is just poached blackberries, blueberries, red currants, black currants, strawberries and raspberries in a warm Stock Syrup (see p.217). The flavors and colors together are fantastic.

And here's just one more extra flavor. Use scissors to cut some thin strips of mint leaves and add them to the syrup. You get a lovely sweet mint flavor with every bite!

Of course, the best accompaniment to fresh fruit salad is simply whipped cream or even homemade Vanilla Ice Cream (see p.190).

SERVES 4

2 apples, peeled and cored	½ cantaloupe or honeydew melon
¾ cup fresh pineapple chunks	1 large orange, segmented
1¼ cups Stock Syrup (either recipe—see p.217)	2 kiwis, peeled and cut into 8 pieces each
2 plums, each cut into 8 segments	12 strawberries or raspberries
1 mango	1 banana, sliced

Cut the apples into 12 segments and mix them with the pineapple chunks. Bring the stock syrup to the boil and pour on to the apple and pineapple. While the syrup is still warm, add the plums. The mix should now be left to cool to room temperature.

Peel the mango, then cut it in half, removing the pit. Cut the mango into chunks. Repeat the same cutting process for the melon. Add the mango, melon, orange and kiwi to the other fruits in the syrup.

The fruit salad is now ready. The strawberries, raspberries and banana should not be added until the salad is going to be served.

Ice Creams

These recipes could just go on and on – there are so many different ice creams and sorbets. They all eat well as desserts on their own or as accompaniments for other dishes.

Most of these recipes are derivatives of a basic vanilla ice cream. In the vanilla recipe, a vanilla bean is used. This gives the ice cream a real vanilla taste and when split and scraped leaves a black speckled finish to the cream. This can be substituted by using a few drops of strong vanilla extract or if you keep some sugar in an airtight container with a vanilla bean the vanilla aroma and flavor will stay with the sugar.

In most of the other ice cream recipes, I suggest that you leave out the vanilla. The quantity of ingredients given in the basic vanilla recipe can, of course, be halved and all the other recipes can follow suit.

If you don't have an ice cream machine, the mix can be left in a bowl and placed in the freezer, making sure it is stirred every 10-15 minutes until set.

If you're in a real hurry, there are a few short-cuts you can try for any of the recipes. You can buy a good quality vanilla ice cream and add the other flavors so it's almost homemade.

Vanilla Ice Cream

This is the base ice cream which you can vary in an infinite number of ways!

SERVES 4–8

1¼ cups heavy whipping cream
1¼ cups milk
1 vanilla bean or a few drops of vanilla
    extract

6 egg yolks
¾ cup sugar

Mix together the cream and milk in a pan. Split the vanilla bean lengthwise and scrape the insides into the milk and cream, then add the scraped bean. Bring to the boil.

While they are heating, beat the egg yolks and sugar together until pale and light. This can be done in a food mixer. Pour on the milk and cream, stirring all the time until well blended. Stir from time to time until the ice cream mix has cooled. Remove the vanilla bean.

Once cooled, the mix is ready to be churned in the ice cream maker. If you have made the full recipe, you'll need to churn it in two batches. Pour the mix into the machine and begin to churn. The ice cream will take about 20–30 minutes and will have thickened and increased in volume. Don't leave the mix churning until completely frozen and set as this will be over-churned and slightly grainy in texture. Take out when thick and starting to freeze and then finish in the freezer. This will give you a lovely silky smooth texture.

If you don't have an ice cream machine, simply pour the mixture into a freezer tray or bowl and freeze, stirring regularly until set.

Clockwise, starting from the top right:
Vanilla Ice Cream; Toffee Ice Cream (see p.200);
Maple Syrup and Pecan Nut Ice Cream (see p.197);
Coconut Ice Cream (see p.195);
Raspberry Soft Fruit Ice Cream (see p.204);
Chocolate Ice Cream (see p.193).

Banana Ice Cream

Try this ice cream with Chocolate Sauce (see p.216) and warm pancakes.

SERVES 4-8

1 recipe Vanilla Ice Cream (see p.190)   1-2 tablespoons banana liqueur
2 large ripe bananas   (optional)
A few drops of lemon juice

First you need to make the vanilla ice cream base. Once made and still warm, peel and chop the bananas and toss them in the lemon juice to help them keep their color. Then add them to the base. This can now be puréed in a food processor or blender and then pushed through a sieve. Stir in the liqueur, if using. The ice cream can now be finished in an ice cream machine, then frozen.

Chocolate Ice Cream

This is a delicious ice cream with lots of very adult alternatives (see p.191)!

SERVES 4-8

1 recipe Vanilla Ice Cream (see p.190), made with ½ cup sugar and without the vanilla bean

6 oz (175 g) good quality semi-sweet chocolate, grated

Follow the vanilla base recipe using only ½ cup of sugar. Once the milk and cream have been brought to the boil, pour onto the grated chocolate and stir. This will melt the chocolate. Taste before churning to check the chocolate flavor is strong enough. Continue with the basic recipe.

Variations

This ice cream has many alternatives:

1. Add some rum to taste.
2. Add some Cointreau or Grand Marnier to taste.
3. Add 2-3 tablespoons of marmalade for chocolate and orange ice cream (and maybe a little Cointreau too!).
4. Add some broken Honeycomb (see p.208) just at the end of churning.

Christmas Pudding Ice Cream

This is a great Christmas pudding alternative to surprise your guests. It eats really well on its own or as an accompaniment to a tart or flan. The other great way to use this recipe is to make it from your left-over pudding, churning it into a new dish.

At Christmas-time, Christmas puddings are available for sale in many North American grocery stores. Keep your eye out for them!

SERVES 4-8

1 lb (450 g) Christmas pudding   5 cups Custard Sauce (see p.215)

The Christmas pudding can be used straight from the package. All you need to do is simply cut the pudding into slices and then into small rough dice. If you are using the left-overs from Christmas lunch, then just break it down into crumble pieces. Now all you have to do is stir in the custard and mix for a minute or two. Pour some of the mix into an ice cream machine (making sure the Christmas pudding pieces are equally distributed) and allow to churn. Once the cream has started to thicken and cream, pour the ice cream into a bowl and finish setting in the freezer. If you over-churn the ice cream it will break down the Christmas pudding and become darker and slightly bitter in taste. Repeat the same process for the remaining mix.

To re-create the pudding theme and shape, just set the ice cream in a pudding basin and freeze. Once turned out, you have a Christmas pudding with a difference! I also like to pour maple syrup over the top to enrich it even more.

If you don't have an ice cream maker, pour the mix onto a tray and set in the freezer, stirring from time to time until frozen. The ice cream doesn't quite have the full volume or texture but still tastes good.

Coconut Ice Cream

This ice cream can take on loads of combinations (see p.191). It can be coated in chocolate, almost like making your own "taste of paradise," mixed with chopped pineapple, made into a Piña Colada ice cream, or even served with Pineapple Fritters (see p.148) and Chocolate Sauce (see p.216). If you don't have a fresh coconut, just replace it with ⅔ cup of dried coconut.

SERVES 4-8

¼ fresh coconut
¾ cup heavy whipping cream
1 cup milk

½ cup sugar
5 egg yolks
1 cup coconut milk

Crack the coconut and peel off a quarter of the white coconut flesh. Chop the flesh finely and mix with the cream and milk. Bring to the boil. While the milk mix is coming to the boil, whisk the sugar and egg yolks together in a large bowl until pale and light. Pour over the boiling milk, then place the bowl over a pan of hot water and stir until thickened. Purée in a blender or processor until the coconut is shredded, then leave to cool. Add the coconut milk and churn in the ice cream machine until beginning to freeze, then pour into a freezer container and freeze until firm.

If you don't have an ice cream maker, pour the mix onto a tray and set in the freezer, stirring from time to time until frozen.

Crème Fraîche Ice Cream

Using crème fraîche in any ice cream really lifts the taste of other flavors. But using it as a main flavoring gives a basic vanilla ice cream a really good bite. For every 1¼ cups of Vanilla Ice Cream (see p.190) you will need to add at least ⅔ cup of crème fraîche while the mixture is still liquid. This will give quite a strong taste. After that it's really up to you. If you want it stronger, simply start to add a spoonful at a time until you have the flavor you want. To make the flavor a little sharper, then also add 1 tablespoon of plain yogurt to the mix.

Honey and Whisky Ice Cream

It is up to you how much whisky you like to add to this adult dessert – I use about two measures.

SERVES 4-8

1 recipe Vanilla Ice Cream (see p.190), made without sugar (vanilla bean optional)	1 (12 oz) (350 g) jar clear honey Whisky to taste

This is really easy to make. Simply mix the honey with the egg yolks from the vanilla recipe and beat them together. Follow the method, adding the whisky to taste before churning.

Lemon Curd Ice Cream

This ice cream is lovely and rich and eats beautifully as a dessert on its own or as an extra for a Steamed Lemon Sponge Cake (see p.156). The ice cream is superb if totally homemade, but also works very well if you substitute the fresh lemon curd for a jar of lemon curd.

SERVES 4-6

1 recipe Lemon Curd (see p.208) or   2 large tablespoons crème fraîche
   1 (12 oz) (350 g) jar of lemon curd   1 large tablespoon plain yogurt

Mix the cooled lemon curd with the crème fraîche and yogurt and churn into ice cream. It's as simple as that!

Maple Syrup and Pecan Nut Ice Cream

You need to make the base with less sugar so that the maple syrup does not make the ice cream too rich (see p. 191).

SERVES 6-8

1 recipe Vanilla Ice Cream (see p.190),   1 cup maple syrup
   using only ⅓ cup of sugar (vanilla   ½-¾ cup chopped pecan nuts
   bean optional)

Follow the recipe and method of the vanilla ice cream using half the sugar quantity. This will allow the sweetness of the maple syrup to work without becoming over-rich. Once the vanilla base is made and cooled, add the maple syrup and begin to churn the ice cream. The pecan nuts should only be added to the mix during the last few minutes of churning. If they are added too early, the nuts will break down and also discolor the cream.

Marmalade Ice Cream

This ice cream is rich, tasty and wonderful! It goes really well with Steamed Orange Sponge Cake (see p.158) or Chocolate Sponge Cake (see p.160). It's best to buy a good quality coarse marmalade to give a strong orange taste.

SERVES 6-8

1 recipe Vanilla Ice Cream (see p.190), made without the vanilla bean

1 (12 oz) (350 g) jar coarse marmalade

Follow the recipe for vanilla ice cream. Stir the boiled cream and milk into the egg yolks and sugar, then add the marmalade and then continue to follow the method.

There's always time for a cup of tea.

Rice Pudding Ice Cream with Raspberry Jam Sauce

I love baked rice pudding. It was one of my favorites at home with the lovely skin on top. Creamed rice pudding is also one of my favorites, especially with raspberry jam spooned on top. Well, I thought I would come up with the opposite. Rice pudding ice cream with warm jam sauce. It works really well and when you tell your guests they've got rice pudding and jam sauce, this will definitely surprise them. This ice cream also works very well in a Rice Pudding Arctic Roll with Raspberry Coulis (see p.205).

SERVES 4–8

For the Rice Pudding

2½ cups milk
1 tablespoon unsalted butter

3 tablespoons sugar
⅓ cup short-grain rice

For the Ice Cream

2½ cups Vanilla Ice Cream (see p.190),
   made with a pinch of freshly grated

nutmeg and without the vanilla bean
or vanilla extract

For the Raspberry Jam Sauce

⅔ cup raspberry jam

2-3 tablespoons water

For the Rice Pudding, bring the milk, butter and sugar to the boil. Add the rice and bring to the simmer. Simmer and cook gently, stirring frequently, until the rice is over-cooked; this will take about 25-30 minutes. The rice has to be close to breaking/purée point to prevent it from becoming crunchy when made into ice cream.

Once the rice dessert has cooled, mix with the vanilla base and churn in the ice cream machine for 15-20 minutes until thickened and increased in volume. The rice pudding ice cream can now be set in the freezer.

To make the sauce, just warm the jam and water together until they reach a thick sauce consistency. If the jam is still too thick, then add a little more water to correct the consistency. The sauce can also be pushed through a sieve to leave a smooth, clear jam sauce ready to be poured over the creamy rich ice cream.

Strawberry or Raspberry Ripple Ice Creams

These are lovely, homemade ripple ices that make a delicious dessert served in a Tuile Cookie basket (see p.176) with fresh cream or Custard Sauce (see p.215). The ice cream has a wonderful flavor with the tartness of the raspberry or strawberry to excite your tastebuds. The quantities to follow are two-thirds ice cream to one-third fruit, so whatever amount you want, if you follow these guidelines it will always work. This ice cream works very well in an Arctic Roll (see p.205).

SERVES 4-8

2 cups Vanilla Ice Cream (see p.190)   ⅔ cup Raspberry or Strawberry Coulis
                                              (see p.207)

Make the ice cream, churn the mixture and place in a freezer container. Spoon the coulis on top and then lightly fold the coulis into the ice cream. This will give you red streaks through the ice cream. Set in the freezer.

Toffee Ice Cream

Here's another use for my simple toffee mix (see p.191).

SERVES 4-8

2½ cups Vanilla Ice Cream (see p.190)   1 (14 oz) (400 g) can of toffee
                                              (see p.164)

Follow the recipe for vanilla ice cream, stirring in the toffee once you have made the custard. Turn the mix in an ice cream machine.

Chocolate and Toffee Ice Cream Sundae

The combinations for this sundae are unlimited and that's the beauty of cooking, there're no limits! So rather than give you a strict recipe, I'll just give you some ideas of how it can be put together. It's best to make it in tall glasses or deep bowls.

Remember, to make this dish you don't have to go through the process of making every component. Most, if not all, of these can be found in most food stores, and you can vary the ingredients however you like.

To make chocolate shavings, take a bar of good, rich dark chocolate and turn it on its side, looking at the width of the bar. From top to bottom scrape along the chocolate with the edge of a palette knife. This will create shavings to sprinkle on top of your desserts.

SERVES as many as you need.

Chocolate Fudge Cake (see p.168) or
   chocolate sponge cake
Pecan Nut Sauce (see p.168)
Chocolate Ice Cream (see p.193)
Toffee Ice Cream (see p.200)
Chocolate Sauce (see p.216)

Heavy whipping cream, whipped
Flaked almonds, toasted
Chocolate shavings
Sprigs of fresh mint to decorate
Confectioners' sugar for sprinkling
Wafer cookies to serve

Dice the cake into ½ inch (1 cm) pieces and mix them with some of the pecan nut sauce. Spoon the cake into the glasses. Next spoon some chocolate ice cream on top and follow that with some toffee or vanilla ice cream. Pour cold chocolate sauce on top. Cover with whipped cream and sprinkle over the toasted almonds and chocolate shavings. This sundae can now be served with a sprig of mint on top, a dusting of confectioners' sugar, a long spoon and a cookie. How does that sound?

Black Forest Arctic Roll

Black Forest Cake is still a popular dessert. The flavors of chocolate, cherries and cream marry well – if the dessert is well made! With this dish I've taken all those flavors and churned them into a tasty and fun dessert. The cake can also be used for a chocolate jelly roll. You'll need a cylinder in which to freeze the ice cream into shape. I use a piece of plastic piping from a hardware store, about 6 inches (15 cm) long by 2½ inches (6 cm) diameter. Wrap plastic film securely round one end. The whole dish might sound a bit involved, but you can save time by using a ready-made ice cream and canned cherries if you like, so have a go!

SERVES 4–6

For the Chocolate Sponge Cake

3 eggs
⅓ cup sugar
½ cup all-purpose flour

5 teaspoons cornstarch
¼ cup unsweetened cocoa powder

For the Arctic Roll

6-8 oz (175-225 g) fresh cherries or
    canned cherries
¼ cup Stock Syrup (see p.217)
Kirsch (optional)

2½ cups Vanilla Ice Cream, prepared
    and churned (see p.190)
3-4 tablespoons black cherry jam

Pre-heat the oven to 350°F (180°C) and grease and line a jelly roll pan.

Whisk the eggs and sugar together until pale and fluffy. Sift together the dry ingredients, then fold into the egg mix a little at a time. Spread the mix evenly in the prepared pan and bake in the pre-heated oven for 10-15 minutes. No color is needed on this sponge cake, just set the mix. Allow to cool.

Pit the cherries and sit them in a pan with the syrup and a splash of kirsch, if using. Bring the cherries to the simmer and cook for 1-2 minutes. Leave to cool. Once cooled, mix half the cherries with the vanilla ice cream. Stand the cylinder up, making sure the base has been well covered with plastic wrap. Spoon the ice cream into the cylinder and set in the freezer.

Sieve the liquid from the remaining cherries and bring the syrup to the boil with the cherry jam. The liquid will now be a lot thicker. Mix the cherries with the syrup.

Turn the chocolate sponge cake off the pan but leave it still attached to the paper. Brush the sponge cake with some cherry jam. Remove the plastic wrap from one end of the ice cream and pour hot water onto the cylinder to loosen and remove the ice cream. Sit the ice cream on the sponge cake and roll until the sponge cake meets, creating a cylinder and cutting off any excess. Roll the whole thing in plastic wrap and freeze for 30 minutes.

To serve, remove from the freezer and take off the plastic wrap before cutting into portions. Each plate can be garnished with a spoon of cherries in syrup.

Variations

To add an extra garnish for a special occasion, simply shape some whipped cream and scrape a palette knife across some dark or milk chocolate to garnish with rolled pieces. Finish with sprigs of mint and lightly dust with confectioners' sugar.

Black Forest Arctic Roll.

Summer Fruit Ice Cream Sundae

This sundae can be made by the same method as the Chocolate and Toffee Sundae. Instead of using the chocolate sponge cake, sandwich the jelly roll sponge cake (see p.205) with raspberry jam and then cut into dice and place in the bottom of the glass. Spoon in some summer fruits mixed with a Fruit Coulis (see p.207). Next is the ice cream. I like to use two ice creams, starting with some Vanilla (see p.190), then adding more fruits before spooning in some Raspberry or Strawberry Ice Cream (see p.200). Finish the sundae with some more fruits and then whipped cream, chocolate and mint (see p. 147).

It's awesome—good luck!

Soft Fruit Ice Cream

This is quick and easy to make. All you need is a sweet Fruit Purée (see p.207) and some crème fraîche.

Crème fraîche is fresh cream that has been treated with a special culture which almost sours the cream and gives it a longer life. It works really well in ice creams, giving a full flavor.

Soft summer fruits, such as strawberries or raspberries (see p.191), work beautifully in this recipe, but there is no need to wait until the soft fruit season to make them. The easy alternative is simply to take a can of almost any fruit – peaches, pears, blackberries or whatever – and purée them in their own syrup. Add some confectioners' sugar to increase the sweetness, then add 2-3 heaped tablespoons of crème fraîche. Now you have a quick and easy ice cream, just churn it in the machine and it's ready.

SERVES 4

1 recipe Fruit Purée (see p.207) 2-3 heaped tablespoons crème fraîche
⅔ cup Stock Syrup (see p.217)

Mix all ingredients together and churn in an ice cream machine for 15-20 minutes until thick. If you don't have a machine, then spoon into a bowl and freeze, stirring every 5-10 minutes until set.

Rice Pudding Arctic Roll

This recipe is a copy of the Black Forest Arctic Roll. Simply make the Rice Pudding Ice Cream (see p.199) and freeze in the plastic cylinder. Then you can create the Arctic roll with the sponge cake. Strawberry Ripple Ice Cream (see p.200) also works. I'm going to serve it with some Raspberry Coulis (see p.207).

SERVES 4-8

For the Sponge Cake

3 eggs, separated
½ cup sugar

⅔ cup all-purpose flour
3 tablespoons + 1 teaspoon cornstarch

For the Arctic Roll

Raspberry jam
Rice Pudding Ice Cream (see p.199)
Raspberry Coulis (see p.207)
Fresh raspberries (optional)

Heavy whipping cream
1 sprig of fresh mint
Confectioners' sugar, sifted

Pre-heat the oven to 350°F (180°) and butter and line a jelly roll pan.

Whisk the egg yolks and ⅓ cup of sugar together until thick and creamy. Whisk the egg whites with the remaining sugar to a firm meringue. Sift the all-purpose flour and cornstarch together, then lightly fold into the egg yolk mix. Carefully fold in the egg white. Spread the mix into the prepared pan and cook in the pre-heated oven for 15-20 minutes. Remove from the oven and allow to cool.

Spread some raspberry jam on top of the sponge cake, keeping the golden brown top for the outside. Remove the ice cream from the cylinder by running the plastic under hot water for a few seconds. Sit the ice cream on top of the sponge cake and roll around, cutting off any excess cake. Roll in plastic wrap and freeze for at least 30 minutes.

Once frozen, remove the plastic wrap and cut into four portions. Garnish each portion with Raspberry Coulis and fresh raspberries (optional). It's also nice served with thick fresh cream, a sprig of mint and lightly dusted with confectioners' sugar.

Fruit Sorbets

Sorbets are a light and refreshing alternative to ice cream. They are good to have as a middle course palate cleanser or as a dessert.

You can use any soft fruits you like – strawberries, raspberries, pineapple, mango, melon – and whichever stock syrup you prefer.

SERVES 4-8

8 oz (225 g) fruit
⅔ cup Stock Syrup (see p.217)

Juice of ½ lemon

Simply mix the fruits with the syrup and purée in a blender, then push through a sieve. You now have a fruit syrup. Add the lemon juice to this to help lift the flavors. Churn in an ice cream machine for 20 minutes and freeze, or turn into a freezer tray and place in the freezer, stirring every 20-30 minutes until frozen.

Variations

If you want to make an apple or pear sorbet, simply peel, core and chop the fruits, mix with the lemon juice and cook in the stock syrup until softened. Then purée and push through a sieve and leave to cool before making into sorbet.

Chocolate Sorbet

You're going to love this recipe. It's easy to make, rich in taste and also very refreshing.

¼ cup unsweetened cocoa
2 cups water

5 oz (150 g) good quality semi-sweet
chocolate
⅔ cup sugar

Simmer the cocoa in the water for 5 minutes. While simmering, chop the chocolate. Pour the water and cocoa onto the chocolate and sugar and stir in. Once cool, churn in the ice cream machine until thickened, then freeze.

Fruit Purées or Coulis

Fruit purées, or coulis, are used for many things, particularly bases for sorbets, as sweet sauces and as flavorings in mousses. The French term coulis *literally means sieved and this method is used for soft fruits such as strawberries, raspberries and black currants. Because of the sharpness in the flavor, the fruits need to be mixed with confectioners' sugar. These quantities are good guidelines; you can vary them to suit the tartness of the fruit. They go very well with ice creams and iced parfaits.*

MAKES about 8 oz (225 g)

8 oz (225 g) soft fruit
½ cup confectioners' sugar, sifted

A few drops of lemon juice

Purée the fruit and sugar together in a food processer or blender, then push through a sieve. If the flavor is still too tart, simply add more confectioners' sugar to taste. The consistency will be of a thick sauce which can be thinned down if needed with some Stock Syrup (see p.217), or some more confectioners' sugar blended with a little water. A few drops of lemon juice will help lift the flavor of the fruit.

Honeycomb

Honeycomb is, of course, the filling in a Crunchie bar. This recipe could be used to make your own, but I like to break the honeycomb into pieces and add it to a chocolate ice cream just at the end of churning. This gives you a lovely crunchy texture in the ice cream. It's also nice just broken and sprinkled on top of an ice cream dessert.

To make honeycomb you need to boil the sugar, so do take care as it reaches very high temperatures. You must always make sure that you have a very clean, large pan for this recipe and also a sugar thermometer will be needed.

SERVES 4-6

2 tablespoons water	2 tablespoons light molasses
1½ cups demerara or light brown sugar	1 tablespoon unsalted butter
1 cup granulated sugar	1 tablespoon baking soda

Pour the water into a saucepan, add the sugars, molasses and butter. Bring the mix to the boil and continue to cook to a small crack temperature. This is 280–284°F (138°–140°C). The sugar mix will have a rich golden color. Add the baking soda; this will lift the sugar and create a light airy texture. Pour the honeycomb mix into a greased 9 × 11 inch (23 × 28 cm) tray and allow to set. Once cooled and set the honeycomb is ready and can be kept in an airtight container.

Lemon Curd

Lemon curd eats very well just on toast or teacakes. I like to use it for Lemon Curd Ice Cream (see p.197) or as a sauce for steamed sponge cakes.

This recipe is very rich with a high butter content. If you prefer, you can cut the butter down to ½ cup (8 tablespoons) and also cut down by 1 egg yolk. The lemon curd will still work without being over-rich and will have a slightly more fluid consistency. There are two alternative methods.

1 cup sugar	Finely grated zest and juice of 3 lemons
1 cup (16 tablespoons) unsalted butter	5 egg yolks

For method 1, put the sugar, butter, lemon juice and zest in a bowl and stir over a pan of simmering water. Once the butter has melted, beat vigorously until well combined. Beat in the egg yolks and continue to cook and stir for 15-20 minutes until the curd has thickened. Pour into a clean jar and cover with waxed paper or plastic film. Once cooled, seal tightly and keep in the refrigerator. This should keep for at least two weeks.

For method 2, whisk the sugar and egg yolks together until light and creamy. Melt the butter with the lemon zest and juice and add to the mix. Cook, stirring, in a bowl over a pan of simmering water until thickened; this will also take about 15-20 minutes.

Lemon Jelly

This is a simple homemade jelly. The lemon jelly goes very well with ice cream. I like to serve either the Vanilla (see p.190), Lemon Curd (see p.197) or Crème Fraîche Ice Cream (see p.196) with it. This is really a good, fun dessert to offer your guests at a dinner party – jelly and ice cream!

The recipe also works well if the lemons are replaced or mixed with limes for a different flavor.

2½ cups water	Finely grated zest and juice of 5 lemons
1⅓ cups sugar	7-8 teaspoons gelatin powder

Warm and dissolve the sugar in 2 cups water on the stove with the lemon juice and zest. Keep on the heat for 2-3 minutes. Remove from the stove. Soak the gelatin in 2½-3 tablespoons cold water for 10 minutes. Stir the gelatin into the warm, sweet lemon water until dissolved. The sweet jelly water can now be left to cool, stirring occasionally. Once cooled, the jelly can be poured into a presentation bowl and left to set in the refrigerator.

Homemade Blackberry Jam

In this recipe there are two alternatives for the quantity of sugar, but both work by the same method. The difference is quite simple. If equal amounts of sugar and fruit are used, more syrup is made from the sugar. Also, by using a preserving sugar containing pectin, the jam is guaranteed to set. By using half the sugar content, less syrup is made and so consequently a thicker more "jammy" texture and not quite as sweet taste is the result. I prefer to make the jam with half of the sugar content to achieve a stronger natural taste of the fruits, although jam made in this way will only last for a maximum of two weeks.

This is a basic recipe which can be applied to most soft fruits such as raspberries, strawberries and cherries. However, sharp, firmer fruits, such as black currants, will require more sugar to balance the acidity.

These berries obviously have seeds so if you prefer to make jam without them, simply strain through a sieve once.

If you intend to eat the jam within a week or two, simply allow the jam to cool, place in warmed jam jars, leave to cool, then chill. The sugar and pectin are both natural preservatives so the jam will keep perfectly fresh.

If you want to store the jams for longer, you'll need to sterilize them. Sterilize the jars first by covering them with cold water in a large pan, then bringing the water to the boil. Leave to boil for 10–15 minutes, then remove and dry. The glass should be warm before adding the hot jam to prevent the jar from shattering. Once the jars are filled, covered and sealed, you can sterilize them further by sitting the jars on a wire rack or cloth in a large pan and almost covering with water. Bring the water to the boil, then repeat the process. Store the jam in a cool, dark place, or chill it; it will last almost indefinitely.

Makes about 2 lb (900 g)

2 lb (900 g) blackberries	Juice of 1 lemon
1 lb (450 g) or 2 lb (900 g) sugar with pectin	

Carefully rinse the blackberries, making sure you do not damage the fruits. Warm the sugar in a large, heavy-based pan over a low heat; this will take 1–2 minutes. Add the fruits and the sugar will begin to dissolve. Once some liquid is forming, turn up the heat and bring to the boil, stirring gently. Stir in the lemon juice. As the mix is heating, some froth and impurities will begin to rise to the top. This froth should be skimmed off. Once boiling rapidly, continue to cook for about 6-7 minutes. The jam should have reached the temperature of 220°F (105°C). With the pectin in the sugar this will be at setting point. If you don't have a sugar thermometer, simply sit a spoonful of mix on a saucer and set in the refrigerator. Once cold and touched, the jam should have a jellied, wrinkled texture and is now ready to pour into the jars and cover with waxed paper. Allow to cool before closing the lids. The jam should be kept in a dark, cool place or chilled for extra life.

Shortcrust and Sweet Crust Pastry

This recipe really is short! In ingredients and in texture.
This recipe is really the minimum amount to make for a good texture. The beauty of this pastry is that it freezes so well to be used later.

MAKES about 14 oz (400 g)

¾ cup (12 tablespoons) unsalted butter,   4 tablespoons cold water
   chopped
2 cups all-purpose flour

Rub the butter into the flour until a crumble effect is achieved. Add the water and fold in very lightly until the pastry is only just beginning to form and bind. Press the pastry between two sheets of plastic film. The pastry will have a marbled look; this indicates just how short the pastry is going to be.

Variations

This pastry works very well with the Fillet of Mackerel with Caramelized Onions and Sweet Peppers (see p.26) or as a savory or sweet tart base. To make sweet pastry, simply add ½ cup of sifted confectioners' sugar to the flour.

Puff Pastry

This recipe is useful for all kinds of desserts and for savory pies as well. It's very satisfying to make your own pastry, but you can resort to the refrigerated section of your supermarket if you are short of time.

Makes about 1 lb (450 g)

1 cup (16 tablespoons) unsalted butter	⅔ cup cold water
1¾ cups all-purpose flour	A few drops of lemon juice
A pinch of salt	

Cut off 4 tablespoons of the butter, melt it then leave it to cool. The remaining block should be left out to soften. Sift the flour and salt together into a large bowl and make a well in the center. Pour the water, lemon juice and cooled, melted butter into the well in the flour and gently fold in the flour to make a pliable dough. Wrap in plastic film and allow to rest in the refrigerator for 20 minutes.

On a lightly floured board, roll out the pastry from four sides, leaving a lump in the center. The dough should look like a crossroads. The remaining block of butter should have softened to a similar texture to the dough; it should be easy to roll without melting but not so hard that it will break the pastry.

Sit the butter on the center lump of the dough (A) and fold over each pastry flap (B). Pat the pastry into a 12 × 6 inch (30 × 15 cm) rectangle and leave to rest in the refrigerator for 10-15 minutes.

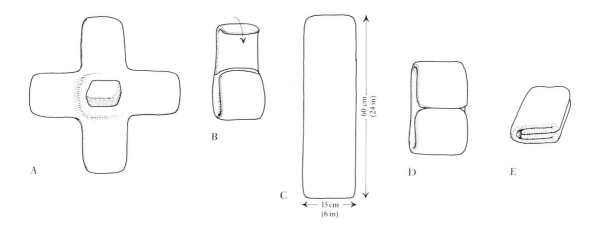

A   B   C   D   E

60 cm
(24 in)

15 cm
(6 in)

Roll out the pastry lengthwise to make it double in length to about 24 inches (60 cm) but the same width (C). Fold in both ends to the center (D) and then fold once more (E). This is called a double turn and should be completed a further three times, each time rolling out the same length and then finishing with a double turn. Always roll with the folded edge on the left, and always leave to rest for 20-30 minutes in the refrigerator before each turn. The pastry should now be rested for at least 30 minutes in the refrigerator before using.

This puff pastry is perfect for the savory tarts (see p.120). To make the pastry crusts, butter and flour your chosen pans: 1 (10 inch) (25 cm) ring or 6 (4 inch) (10 cm) tart pan(s). Roll the pastry out thinly and line the tart pans, leaving any excess turned over the sides. Sit the pastry lined pans on a baking sheet and rest in the refrigerator for 10-15 minutes. Line with wax or parchment paper and baking beans or rice. Bake in a pre-heated oven at 400°F (200°C) for 15-20 minutes until the pastry is baked and golden. Remove the paper and beans, then use a sharp knife to trim off any excess pastry over the sides, leaving the crusts in the tart pans.

Almond Paste or Frangipane

This almond paste is the recipe which is used to make Bakewell Tart, that old favorite nursery dessert. The mixture freezes well, or you can make it in smaller amounts, just maintaining the same proportions.

SERVES 4-8

1 cup (16 tablespoons) unsalted butter, cold	1½ cups ground almonds
	½ cup all-purpose flour
1 cup sugar	4 eggs

Cream together the butter and sugar until almost white. Mix together the ground almonds and flour. Add one egg at a time to the butter and sugar mixture, sprinkling a handful of ground almonds and flour at the same time. This helps the butter and sugar cream to accept the eggs. Once all the eggs have been added, just continue to fold in the remaining almond and flour mixture.

Cook as directed in the recipes.

Banana and Toffee Cream Crêpes

Here's a great alternative for Shrove Tuesday! Of course, the crêpes can also be used in many other desserts, especially when served with ice creams. How does warm crêpes with vanilla ice cream and hot jam sauce sound?

SERVES 4-6

4 bananas	Confectioners' sugar, sifted
1 recipe Toffee Cream (see p.165)	A few sprigs of fresh mint
Maple syrup (optional)	

For the Crêpes

1 cup all-purpose flour	1¼ cups milk
A pinch of salt	2 tablespoons unsalted butter, melted
1 egg	Vegetable oil

Sift the flour and salt together. Beat the egg into the milk and whisk into the flour. Add the melted butter. The crêpe mix is now ready. Pre-heat a 10 inch (25 cm) pan and trickle some vegetable oil into the pan, making sure the oil has very lightly covered the pan. Add a thin layer of crêpe mix to the pan. Cook for 15-20 seconds until golden, then flip over and cook for a further 10-15 seconds on the other side. The crêpe is now ready. Repeat the same process until all the mix is finished.

Peel the bananas and cut diagonally into thick slices. Sit the crêpes on the plate and fold in half, keeping the semi-circular side facing you. Overlap the banana slices on one quarter of the crêpe and spoon some toffee cream on top. Fold the other half of crêpe over the cream, leaving a triangular-shaped dessert on the plate. Sprinkle with maple syrup, if using, and dust confectioners' sugar around the plate. Garnish with a sprig of mint.

Variations

Try dusting the sliced bananas with confectioners' sugar and glazing them under the broiler until the sugar has caramelized, then use them in the crêpes.

Anglaise (Fresh Custard) Sauces

This recipe is for a fresh custard or anglaise sauce, which can act as a base for so many different flavors. You must only ever serve it warm, not boiled, as this will scramble the egg yolks in the cream mix. The fresh vanilla is optional and can be omitted when using other flavors. To have the flavor of vanilla always at hand, keep a vanilla bean in your jar of sugar; the aroma from the bean will impregnate the sugar.

MAKES 2½ cups (750ml)

8 egg yolks
⅓ cup sugar
1 vanilla bean, split (optional)

1¼ cups milk
1¼ cups heavy whipping cream

Beat the egg yolks and sugar together in a bowl until well blended. Split and scrape the insides of the vanilla bean, if using, into the milk and cream and bring to the boil. Sit the bowl over a pan of hot water and whisk the cream into the egg mix. As the egg yolks warm, the cream will thicken to create a custard. Keep stirring until it coats the back of a spoon. Remove the bowl from the heat. The custard can now be served warm or stirred occasionally until it cools. Serve warm or cold.

Variations

For Lemon Custard Sauce, add the zest of 2 lemons, to the milk and cream when heating, then leave it in the mix throughout the cooking process. Once the custard has thickened, add the juice of one lemon and taste. If the lemon flavor is not strong enough, simply add more lemon juice to taste. Strain the custard through a sieve.

For Orange Custard Sauce, add the zest of 2 oranges to the milk and cream when heating, then cook as for the basic recipe. Orange juice will not be used in this recipe. To lift the flavor of the sauce, try adding a few drops of Cointreau or Grand Marnier.

For Rum Custard Sauce, add some rum to taste at the end of cooking the vanilla custard. This goes very well with Pineapple Fritters (see p.148). Dried coconut could also be added to this recipe during the cooking process and/or coconut milk added at the end.

Coffee Custard Sauce can be made by replacing the vanilla bean with 2 teaspoons of good fresh ground coffee and cook as for the vanilla base recipe. Once the coffee custard has completely cooled just strain through a sieve to remove any excess granules.

Chocolate Sauce

This chocolate sauce is lovely and rich in flavor and texture. It eats really well either hot or cold and goes with so many different desserts. Chocolate must be very carefully treated. If overheated, the chocolate will become split and grainy. Not every commercial chocolate works in cooking, but I have always found Ghiradelli to be quite a safe bet.

SERVES 4-8

7 oz (200 g) good quality semi-sweet chocolate, finely chopped
2 tablespoons unsalted butter, chilled and diced

⅔ cup milk
2 tablespoons heavy whipping cream
2 tablespoons sugar

Mix together the chocolate and butter. Boil the milk, cream and sugar and pour onto the chocolate mix. Stir the mixture until completely melted, but do not allow it to re-boil. The chocolate sauce is now ready. Serve warm or cold – the cooler the temperature, the thicker the sauce.

Stock Syrups

These syrups have many uses. They are a great base for sorbets, for poaching, and for steeping fruits. Any spirits or liqueurs can be added; even teabags or fresh tea can be added for sorbets or ice creams. I'm going to give two recipes. The first is very basic and the second is almost a dish on its own and packed with flavor. Both keep almost indefinitely if chilled. The fruit stock syrup is good to use in a fresh fruit salad and can also have mint added to take on another flavor.

For Simple Stock Syrup

2½ cups water	1½ cups sugar

For Fruit Stock Syrup

2½ cups water	Pared zest and juice of 2 oranges
1½ cups sugar	½ cinnamon stick
Zest and juice of 2 lemons	1 vanilla bean

Whichever syrup you are making, bring all the ingredients to the simmer, stirring to dissolve the sugar, then remove from the heat and allow to cool and infuse.

If you prefer a thicker, sweeter syrup, add an extra ½ cup of sugar. If you are making the fruit stock syrup, it's best to leave the syrup with all ingredients included until needed, and then just drain off.

Stocks, Sauces and Basic Recipes

T his chapter holds the secret to getting full flavor from all my recipes. So set aside a slow Saturday morning and put some of these basics into the freezer to have on hand when cooking. Now I understand that sometimes you need to cook things from a can or package. But do try making some stocks and sauces from scratch—I guarantee that the final flavor is worth your effort.

ABOVE *Preparing Salsa Dressing (see p.243).*
LEFT *A selection of ingredients needed to make the dressings.*

If you don't have time to make your own stocks, I've included some alternatives that are available from most supermarkets—all of them have been tried and tested. There are also some extras here that I picked up on my travels around Britain, such as the Irish Soda Bread.

In this section I have included some miscellaneous dishes. These are recipes that don't really need to be mixed with any particular dish in the rest of the book, but are really good to eat so I decided to include them. There's the homemade Worcestershire sauce, lovely sprinkled on a steak or used to lift a sauce, Bone Marrow Dumplings, a great addition to any stew or soup, and my favorite peanut sauce, which reminds me of when I lived in Amsterdam years ago and was always eating chicken satay sticks with a hot peanut sauce to dip them in. The flavor is hot and spicy, so at your next barbecue have a go!

Fish Stock

To make a good fish stock, you'll need a friendly fishmonger. Halibut and sole bones produce the best stock, giving a good, full taste and clear jelly-like finish. The stock is good for poaching fish and for making fish soups and sauces. (For information on ready-made alternatives, see p.226.)

MAKES about 9 cups

1 large onion, sliced
1 leek, sliced
2 celery stalks, sliced
4 tablespoons unsalted butter
A few fresh parsley stalks
1 bay leaf

6 black peppercorns
2 lb (900 g) halibut or sole bones, washed
1¼ cups dry white wine
10 cups water

Sweat the vegetables in the butter without coloring. Add the parsley stalks, bay leaf and peppercorns. Chop the fish bones, making sure there are no blood clots left on them. Add them to the vegetables and continue to cook for a few minutes. Add the wine and boil to reduce until almost dry. Add the water and bring to a simmer. Allow to simmer for 20 minutes, then drain through a sieve. The stock is now ready to use, or to store for a few days in the refrigerator.

Chicken Stock

Chicken stock is one of our most important bases. It's used for most soups and many cream sauces. It's also very simple to make. I'm sure your local butcher will help you out with some chicken bones. If not, then cook a boiling fowl with vegetables in water and you will have a tasty stock and the bird to eat as well. You'll need a large stock pot, about 2½-3 gallons capacity, but if you don't have one you can easily reduce the quantities. (For information on ready-made alternatives see p.226.)

MAKES 10 cups

2 onions, chopped	1 bay leaf
2 celery stalks, chopped	1 sprig of fresh thyme
2 leeks, chopped	A few black peppercorns
2 tablespoons unsalted butter	4 lb (1.8 kg) chicken carcasses, chopped
1 garlic clove, crushed	15 cups water

In a large stock pot, lightly soften the vegetables in the butter without coloring. Add the garlic, bay leaf, thyme, peppercorns and chopped carcasses. Cover with the cold water and bring to the simmer, skimming all the time. Allow the stock to simmer for 2-3 hours. Strain through a sieve. The stock is now ready to use and will keep well chilled or frozen.

Vegetable Stock

A very similar recipe for vegetable stock is included in the original Rhodes Around Britain *book. This recipe gives a different result. I have increased the quantity of carrots to give a sweeter taste to the stock. It can also be cooked to various stages leaving it at almost full capacity for risottos or vegetable stews, or reducing while cooking for butter sauces.*

MAKES about 3¾ cups

12 oz (350 g) carrots	1 bay leaf
4 celery stalks	1 sprig of fresh thyme
1 large onion	5 cups water
1 leek	Salt and freshly ground black pepper
2 tablespoons unsalted butter	

Roughly chop all the vegetables into ½ inch (1 cm) dice. Melt the butter in a pan and add the vegetables. Cook on a low heat with the bay leaf and thyme for 10-12 minutes until softening. Add the water and bring to the simmer. Continue to simmer for about 20-30 minutes until the stock has reduced to about 3¾ cups. Strain through a sieve. The stock is now ready to use or can be stored for a few days in the refrigerator.

Veal or Beef Stock or *Jus*

This stock is a base to a lot of cooking, and really holds the essence of a good dish. Reading this recipe may well make you want to think twice about it, but it is worth making and so satisfying once made. It will give you great sauces and, of course, will store well in your freezer, so go on – have a go! It is best started in the morning which will allow the stock to cook throughout the day. Ask your butcher for a few beef or veal trimmings to make the stock.

If this really is too much, then a lot of good gravy bases can be found but do use them carefully, not making them too thick and strong. (For information on ready-made alternatives see p.226.)

MAKES about 22½ cups (5½ quarts) or 3¾ cups *jus*

3 onions, halved
2–3 tablespoons water
5 lb (2.25 kg) veal or beef bones
8 oz (225 g) veal or beef trimmings
8 oz (225 g) carrots, coarsely chopped
3 celery stalks, coarsely chopped

1 leek, chopped
3–4 tomatoes, chopped
1 garlic clove, halved
1 bay leaf
1 sprig of fresh thyme

Pre-heat the oven to 225°F (110°C).

Lay the onion halves flat in a roasting pan with the water. Place in the very cool oven and allow to caramelize slowly until they have totally softened and colored. This process will take 1–2 hours. The sugars in the onions will slowly cook and give a wonderful taste. Put the onions on one side.

Increase the oven temperature to 400°F (200°C). Place all the bones and trimmings in a roasting pan and roast for about 30 minutes until well colored. Roast the chopped carrots and celery in another roasting pan for about 20 minutes until lightly colored.

When ready, add the bones, trimmings and vegetables to the onions in the pot along with the leeks, tomatoes, garlic, bay leaf and thyme. Fill the pot with cold water – you'll need about 22½ cups (5½ quarts). Bring the stock to the simmer and skim off any impurities. Allow to cook for 6–8 hours, and with this you will achieve the maximum taste.

When ready, drain and discard the bones and vegetables. This is now your veal stock and you can cool it and freeze it in convenient quantities.

Alternatively, you can make a *jus* from the stock. Allow the liquid to boil and reduce down to about 3¾ cups, skimming occasionally. The stock should be thick and of a sauce consistency. Make sure that you taste all the time during reduction. If the sauce tastes right but is not thick enough, thicken it lightly with cornstarch mixed in water. (Of course, I do hope that won't be necessary!) You now have a veal *jus*, a classic sauce.

Onion Gravy

Serve this classic gravy to accompany sauces or liver dishes.

SERVES 4

8 onions, thinly sliced
2 tablespoons water

2½ cups Veal *Jus* (see p.224) or bought
   alternative (see p.226)

Place the onions in a pan with the water and cook very slowly, stirring all the time. The sugar from the onions will slowly caramelize and become dark golden brown and sweet-tasting. The process will take about 2 hours. Add the veal *jus* and simmer for a further 30 minutes. The gravy will be even richer in taste and color with a lovely, shiny finish.

Alternative Stocks and Sauces

Making fresh stocks at home is not always possible, so I've been out doing some homework on stocks and sauces in search of some good commercial alternatives to make the cooking of some of my dishes a little easier.

Fish and Chicken Stocks

Alternatives to these can be found in the refrigerated section of most quality supermarkets. They are sold in plastic containers each holding about 1¼-1½ cups. The beauty of these is they taste great, they have good color and jelly texture, and they are sold as stocks ready to use. They really are the best I've found, but if you can't get hold of them there are also some good quality bouillon cubes.

Beef and Veal *Jus*

In the basic recipe, these start out as stocks and then for use in other recipes they are reduced to a sauce consistency. I've found a sauce which will cut out all of this, and is an instant *jus* to use as a base sauce in many of the recipes asking for veal or beef *jus*. Au Jus Gravy Mix is made by Knorr in their Gravy Classics line, and should be available in just about every supermarket or good grocery store.

I hope these few suggestions will help. It's always good to have a go at making your own stocks, sauces, jus and pasta, but cooking has to be practical and for regular use the products mentioned above will help tremendously. I certainly think they will make life for you an awful lot easier.

Tasting is an essential part of preparing any dish.

Vegetable Butter Sauce

This is a simple sauce which is easiest to make if you have a food processor or blender.

SERVES 4

⅔ cup reduced Vegetable Stock (see p.223)
4-6 tablespoons unsalted butter at room temperature

Salt and freshly ground white pepper

Pour the vegetable stock into a small pan and add 4 tablespoons of the butter. Bring to the simmer, whisking all the time. Season with salt and pepper. Whisk vigorously or use the food processor or blender and you should have a light creamy consistency. If the sauce seems a little too thin, then simply add the remaining butter and blend once more. The sauce is now ready.

Lemon Butter Sauce

This is one of the simplest possible sauces which has a silky texture and just enough to complement cod and salmon dishes in particular.

SERVES 4-6

1 cup (16 tablespoons) unsalted butter
Juice of 1 lemon

¼ cup Chicken Stock (see p.222) or Vegetable Stock (see p.223)
Salt and freshly ground white pepper

Chop the butter into ½ inch (1 cm) pieces and put it into a pan with the lemon juice and stock. Bring to a simmer, whisking all the time. Do not allow the sauce to boil or the butter will separate. If it is too thick, add more stock. If you like a sharper taste, add more lemon juice. Season with salt and pepper and serve immediately. To give a creamier texture, simply purée the sauce in a food processor or blender.

Fennel Butter Sauce

This is a good sauce for fish. The anise flavor of fennel is helped by the addition of star anise in the cooking liquid. To increase the flavor for a fish dish, use some Fish Stock (see p.221) in the reduction for the sauce. However, you'll find that fennel creates a good stock of its own and when reduced by three-quarters should be strong enough on its own.

SERVES 4

2 fennel bulbs	Salt
3 cups water	1-2 star anise
Juice of 1 lemon	4-6 tablespoons unsalted butter

Trim the root and top stalks from the fennel. Place in boiling water with the lemon juice, star anise and a pinch of salt. Return to the boil, cover the fennel with a wax or parchment paper and simmer until tender; this will take about 20-30 minutes. When ready, a sharp knife will just be able to reach the center of the bulb.

Remove the fennel bulbs, then boil and reduce the cooking liquid down to about ⅔-1¼ cups to give a good, strong taste. Dice the fennel into ¼ inch (5 mm) pieces. The liquid can now be finished with the butter, just whisking it in to create a fennel butter sauce. Remove the star anise. Purée the sauce with a hand blender to give a more creamy texture. Add the fennel and warm through. Check and adjust the seasoning.

Variations

Chopped chives, tarragon or mint could be added to this sauce at the last minute to give it another flavor.

Red Wine Sauce

This sauce tastes good with almost any meat – chicken, beef, pork, veal – and even eats well with baked fish.

MAKES about 5 cups

4 shallots, chopped
1 large carrot, chopped
2 celery stalks, chopped
2 tablespoons unsalted butter
1 garlic clove, crushed
1 bay leaf
1 sprig of fresh thyme

8 oz (225 g) beef skirt or beef
   trimmings (optional)
1 tablespoon olive oil (optional)
1 (750 ml) bottle red wine or 3 cups
5 cups Veal *Jus* (see p.224) or bought
   alternative (see p.226)
Salt and freshly ground white pepper

In a large pan, cook the chopped vegetables in a little butter with the garlic and herbs, allowing them to color. In a frying pan, fry the meat, if used, in the oil, browning on all sides, then add the meat to the vegetables. Pour the red wine into the frying pan to release any flavors from the trimmings. Scrape and stir, then pour the wine onto the meat and vegetables and boil to reduce until almost dry.

Add the veal *jus* and bring to the simmer, skim off any impurities, then simmer the sauce gently for 30 minutes. Pass through a sieve, squeezing all the juices from the vegetables and meat. Check for seasoning and you now have a rich, glistening red wine sauce.

Quick Red Wine Sauce

At work in my restaurant, I always make fresh stocks, gravies and sauces, but when you're at home it's not often or ever possible. But there is always an alternative. Whenever making sauces from packages it's best to add double the quantity of water given in the recipe to give a better consistency. Knorr's classic Brown Gravy or Demi-Glace Sauce Mix is a good one to use. To make the sauce even simpler, you can leave out the shallots, bay leaf and peppercorns.

MAKES about 5 cups

2½ cups red wine
2 shallots, sliced
1 bay leaf

A few black peppercorns
1 package instant gravy made up with
3 cups water

To make this red wine sauce, bring the wine to the boil with the shallots, bay leaf and peppercorns, then boil until reduced by three-quarters, leaving about ⅔ cup of strong red wine. Add the gravy and cook for a few minutes. Strain before serving.

Tomato Coulis

This is a very useful basic for all sorts of recipes.

MAKES about 3¾ cups

1 large onion, chopped
2 celery stalks, chopped
1 large carrot, chopped
1 garlic clove, crushed
A few fresh basil or tarragon leaves or a
    pinch of dried tarragon
1 sprig of fresh thyme or a pinch of
    dried thyme
2 tablespoons olive oil

4 tablespoons unsalted butter
⅔ cup dry white wine
1 lb (450 g) tomatoes, chopped
1¼ cups Chicken Stock (see p.222) or
    Vegetable Stock (see p.223)
1 tablespoon tomato paste
Salt and freshly ground white pepper
A few drops of Spicing Essence (see
    p.233) (optional)

Cook the chopped onion, celery and carrot with the garlic and herbs in the olive oil and butter for a few minutes until softened. Add the white wine and boil to reduce until almost dry. Add the tomatoes and cook for a few minutes, then add the stock and tomato paste, bring to the simmer, cover with a lid and continue to cook for 20 minutes. Purée the sauce, then push it through a sieve to give a smooth sauce consistency. If the sauce is a little thick, add more stock to reach the right consistency. Season to taste with salt and pepper. The coulis is now ready. To make the sauce more spicy, add a few drops of spicing essence at a time, if using, whisking and tasting until you have the flavor you want.

Variations

You can also use this recipe to make a red pepper coulis. Just replace 12 oz (350 g) of the tomatoes with an equal weight of seeded red bell peppers, then follow the same procedure.

Spicing Essence

I think this little trick comes from Escoffier's days; it is often used for spicing up a sauce or other dish. It was also occasionally used to mask the flavors of a meat that wasn't quite right! Well, I'm glad to say that I use it purely for enhancing flavors, and it works its magic particularly with Tomato Coulis (see p.232).

MAKES about ⅔ cup

⅓ cup demerara or light brown sugar   ⅔ cup malt vinegar

Simply dissolve the sugar in the vinegar, then boil for a few minutes until reduced to a syrup. It is now ready to use, and only a few drops are needed to spice your sauces. After that, it can be kept in an airtight jar in the refrigerator for as long as you like.

Tomato Dressing or Sauce

This tomato dressing can also be a thick fresh tomato sauce. When tomatoes are cooking, they create a lot of excess water. This sauce is cooked until almost all the water has evaporated, leaving you with almost a fresh tomato purée. To make the sauce into a dressing, loosen with Basic Vinaigrette (see p.241) or olive oil to taste.

SERVES 4

1 tablespoon unsalted butter
1 tablespoon olive oil
½ onion, finely chopped
1 small garlic clove, crushed
¾ cup white wine

1 lb (450 g) ripe tomatoes, skinned and
  seeded
1 teaspoon tomato paste
Salt and freshly ground black pepper

Melt the butter with the olive oil in a warm pan until the butter begins to bubble. Add the onion and garlic and cook for a few minutes until the onions have softened. Pour the white wine over the onions and bring to the boil. Continue to boil until the wine has reduced and is almost dry.

While this is reducing, chop the tomatoes to a coarse pulp. Add the tomatoes and tomato paste to the pan and bring to the simmer. While the tomatoes are cooking, a lot of water will be created, so allow this to evaporate. Season with salt and pepper and the sauce is ready.

Spicy Tomato Sauce

This sauce goes so well with seafood of all types. It's almost like eating a loose, spicy tomato chutney. Once made, it can be kept chilled for up to two weeks.

MAKES about 1 lb (450 g)

⅓ cup olive oil
3 shallots or 2 onions, finely chopped
2 garlic cloves, crushed
A few fresh basil, thyme and tarragon
    leaves
2 lb (900 g) tomatoes, skinned and
    seeded

2 tablespoons red wine vinegar
1 teaspoon sugar
Salt
2-3 drops of Tabasco sauce

Warm the olive oil in a pan and add the chopped shallots or onions, the garlic and herbs. It's best to have the herbs in sprigs as these can then be easily removed at the end of cooking. Allow the shallots and herbs to cook gently for 4-5 minutes until tender.

Cut the tomato flesh into ¼ inch (5 mm) dice and add to the shallots. Have the pan on a very low heat, just on a light simmer, and cook for about 45 minutes. The sauce may cook a little quicker or take a little longer – this will really depend on the water content of the tomatoes. After 45 minutes, add the wine vinegar and sugar and cook for a further 15 minutes. The tomatoes should have taken on an almost lumpy sauce texture; if the sauce is very thick, simply fold in a little more olive oil. Allow to cool until just warm, then season with salt and Tabasco.

Pesto Sauce

Pesto sauce can be bought in most supermarkets and food stores, but here is a simple version to make yourself. No Parmesan will be needed for this sauce.

SERVES 4

½ cup pine nuts
⅔ cup olive oil
1 small garlic clove, crushed

1 large bunch of basil
Salt and freshly ground black pepper

Simply brown the nuts lightly in the olive oil, then allow to cool. Add the crushed garlic clove, basil, a pinch of salt and pepper and blend to a purée in a food processor or blender. This is now ready and can be kept for 2–3 days in the refrigerator.

Hollandaise Sauce

This is a quick way of making a French classic.

MAKES about 1 cup

1 cup (16 tablespoons) unsalted butter
2 egg yolks
1 tablespoon warm water

Juice of ½ lemon
Salt and cayenne pepper or freshly
    ground white pepper

Melt the butter in a pan, then leave it to cool slightly so that it is just warm when added to the sauce; if it is too hot, the sauce will curdle. The butter will have separated, so you will only be adding the butter oil to the sauce. This is clarified butter.

Add the egg yolks to the water in a bowl and whisk over a pan of hot water until cooked and thickened. Remove from the heat and add the clarified butter, whisking until the sauce is thick. Add the lemon juice and season with salt and cayenne or white pepper.

Worcestershire Sauce

I enjoy finding, trying and hopefully developing recipes like this. I looked through a lot of old cookbooks to find this so that I could have a go at matching the famous bottle we all know and use. Well, it's not quite the same, and you can't really match that distinctive taste, but it's fun and interesting to make, especially when you have to wait a few weeks for the result!

The Worcestershire sauce recipe must be 160 years old. The recipe was found and given to the makers in India. They soon discovered how popular the sauce was and I don't think they ever looked back.

MAKES 3¾ cups

2½ cups malt vinegar	A pinch of cayenne
⅔ cup ketchup	A pinch of ground cinnamon
2 tablespoons anchovy paste	1 garlic clove, crushed
2 shallots or 1 onion, finely chopped	A pinch of freshly grated nutmeg
3 tablespoons soy sauce	A pinch of ground cardamom
	A pinch of salt

There are a few ways of putting this recipe together.

The first is simply to mix all the ingredients and keep in an airtight bottle or container for 2-3 weeks, making sure the bottle is shaken every day.

Another way is to mix all the liquid ingredients with the onion and garlic, bring to the boil and simmer for 30 minutes before adding the spices and salt. Bottle and cool, make airtight and keep for two weeks, shaking every day.

The mix can also be made without the herbs, just mixing the liquids and onion. This will still need to be left and shaken every day for 2-3 weeks.

After the marinating period, strain the sauce before use.

Note

I have used tomato ketchup in this recipe because it is readily available to North American cooks. However, if you ever spot walnut or mushroom ketchup, that will give you a more authentic flavor.

Peanut Sauce

This is the sauce that you find in Thai restaurants served with chicken or pork satay. It's a good sauce to go with barbecued chicken pieces or wings, such as my recipe on page 51. You can follow the recipe with lemon and paprika, marinate simply in lime juice, or just plain grill the chicken. You can lift the flavors in the peanut sauce with a dash of lime juice, too.

SERVES 4

1 cup crunchy peanut butter
3 garlic cloves, crushed
15 fresh cilantro leaves
¼ cup soy sauce

2 tablespoons Japanese sake
¼–½ teaspoon chili oil
½ cup coconut milk
Water

In a food processor, blend the peanut butter with the garlic and cilantro. In a separate jug, mix the soy sauce, sake, chili oil and coconut milk. With the motor running, pour the mixture slowly into the processor until all the liquid has blended in. The sauce should be thick but not set like peanut butter. If the sauce is too thick, just loosen it by adding a tablespoon of water at a time. The sauce can be served warmed or kept chilled for 2–3 days.

Cranberry *Jus* or Gravy

The flavor of this sauce can be helped by taking a good handful of vegetable mirepoix (roughly chopped carrots, shallots or onions, celery and leeks) and cooking them with 2 bay leaves and a sprig of fresh thyme for a few minutes before adding the red wine. The sauce will then need to be sieved before adding the cranberry sauce.

SERVES 4–8

1½ cups red wine
2½ cups Veal *Jus* (see p.224) or
    alternative (see p.226)

2 large tablespoons Cranberry Sauce
    (see p.239)

Boil the red wine until reduced by two-thirds. Add the veal *jus* or alternative and bring the sauce to the simmer. Add the cranberry sauce and continue to simmer gently for 10-15 minutes. Stir in the cranberry sauce until well blended.

Variations

To make a quick cranberry-flavored sauce just take 2½ cups of *jus* alternative (see p.226) and add 2 tablespoons of bought or homemade cranberry jelly. More can be added to adjust the taste to your liking.

Cranberry Sauce with Orange

The obvious main ingredient here is, of course, the cranberries. Cranberry sauce can be made with just cranberries, sugar and a little water, but I replace the water with orange juice, and spice it with a little port; a combination that has become a classic. I also like to add a little chopped shallot to help the savory taste of the dish.

This sauce eats very well with roast turkey, pork or game and with any of the bubble and squeak variations. It's also good to serve with cold meats and pies.

SERVES 4

1 lb (450 g) fresh cranberries
½ cup sugar
Juice of 2 large oranges

½ teaspoon very finely chopped shallots
¾ cup port

Simply place all the ingredients in a pan and bring to a simmer. Cook gently for 10-15 minutes until the cranberries are just beginning to break.

Vinegars and Oils

Malt vinegar is probably the best known, especially for sprinkling on your "fish and chips!" Malt vinegar is made from malted barley (as, of course, is whisky!), and gets its color from caramel. The strongest of vinegars, it is used mostly for pickling, and I've often used it in chutney recipes where it helps to achieve the right acidity for the ingredients. Don't use it in basic dressings as its strength is just too much for salads.

Red and white wine vinegars are the ones to use for most general dressings and purposes. Red wine vinegar is the best. Wine vinegars are allowed to mature slowly in barrels until the vinegars have turned the alcohol into acetic acid. They can be made more swiftly by heating, but this tends to destroy some of the flavors.

Balsamic vinegar must be the most used vinegar in modern cookery, which doesn't surprise me as it really is astounding. There are many cheap copies on the market which aren't worth buying. Real balsamic vinegar is made from Trebbiano grapes and should be a minimum of five years old to have any true flavor. The older it gets, the better and stronger it tastes but, of course, the more expensive it is to buy. Twelve-year-old balsamic is a great medium and although it's pricey, you need very little because of its immense flavor. Some balsamics can be as old as forty years, but this is very rare and you'll probably have to wait another forty years to try one!

Oils

The oils that I generally use are extra-virgin olive oil and peanut oil.

*Peanut is a very basic oil which is used in France (*huile à l'arachide*) as a base in most dressings and in frying. It's very similar to sunflower oil and has quite a bland flavor. In basic dressings I mix it with olive oil, which prevents the dressing from becoming too overpowering. It is also cheaper to make and works well on all simple salads.*

Virgin olive oil is an oil from the first pressing which is totally pure, without any heating or chemical processing. The "extra" in front applies to its low acidity grade. Extra-virgin oil has 1 percent acidity, which is the lowest and the best.

Basic Vinaigrette

This basic recipe is very convenient. Once made, it can sit in your refrigerator and be used at any time and for any dish you might fancy. The vinegar just gives a very slight sweetness to the taste.

MAKES 2½ cups

1¼ cups extra-virgin olive oil (French or Italian)
1¼ cups peanut oil
2 tablespoons balsamic vinegar
1 bunch of fresh basil
½ bunch of fresh tarragon

3-4 sprigs of fresh thyme
12 black peppercorns, lightly crushed
3 shallots, finely chopped
2 garlic cloves, crushed
1 bay leaf
1 teaspoon coarse sea salt

Warm the olive and peanut oils together. Place all the remaining ingredients into a 2½ cups bottle. Pour the oil into the bottle and close with a cork or screw top. For the best results, leave to marinate for a week, which will allow the flavors to enhance the oils. To help the dressing along, shake the bottle once a day. Taste for seasoning before use.

Red Wine Vinaigrette

This is a basic recipe to which you can add your favorite herbs. The best to use, unchopped, are basil, tarragon or thyme. When you are going to use the dressing just add some chopped fresh chives, basil, thyme or tarragon to finish the dressing.

MAKES about 2½ cups

4 shallots or 1 large onion, finely
   chopped
2 garlic cloves, crushed
1¼ cups red wine

1¼ cups red wine vinegar
2 teaspoons Dijon mustard
2 cups olive oil
Salt and freshly ground black pepper

Mix the shallots or onion with the garlic in a pan and add the red wine. Bring to the boil, then boil to reduce until almost dry. Add the red wine vinegar and boil to reduce by three-quarters. Remove the pan from the heat.

While the shallots are still warm, add the Dijon mustard and blend in with the olive oil. Season with salt and pepper. The dressing can now be left to cool and then bottled. Chilled, it keeps for several weeks.

Mayonnaise

Homemade mayonnaise is so much tastier than bought mayonnaise. Use it with potatoes in a salad, or as a dressing for sandwiches.

MAKES about 2½ cups

3 egg yolks
1 tablespoon malt, white wine or
   balsamic vinegar
A pinch of English or Dijon mustard

Salt and freshly ground white pepper
1¼ cups olive oil
1 teaspoon hot water
A few drops of lemon juice (optional)

Whisk the egg yolks, vinegar, mustard and seasonings together, then slowly add the olive oil, whisking continuously. When all the oil has been added, finish with the hot water and correct the seasoning. A few drops of lemon juice can be added to enhance the taste.

Vierge Dressing

This dressing has a very different flavor and lends itself best to fish dishes. I was first inspired to make it whilst staying at La Côte St Jacques in Joigny, France, in the mid 1980s when it was served with a red mullet dish. That restaurant now has three Michelin stars.

MAKES 2½ CUPS

2½ cups extra-virgin olive oil (French or
    Italian)
2 tablespoons coriander seeds, crushed
1 bunch of fresh tarragon

12 black peppercorns, crushed
4 shallots, chopped
2 garlic cloves, crushed
A pinch of sea salt

Warm the olive oil with the coriander seeds. Place the remaining ingredients in a 2 cups screw-top jar and pour the oil and coriander on top. Screw on the lid and leave to marinate for 1 week, shaking the bottle daily.

Salsa Dressing

Salsa is a Mexican relish that has so many variations. It's really a fresh sweet and sour chutney, come sauce, come dressing. Another ingredient is chilies, so not only is it sweet and sour but hot, too! This recipe goes well with hot or cold fish, meats, chicken, or you can even use it as a relish for a hamburger. The most classic version is Salsa Verde, a green chutney with garlic, parsley, mint, mustard, capers, green chilies, oil and vinegar. There are also red salsas and fruit salsas and more, but this we'll just call "Salsa Dressing!"

SERVES 4

2 red onions, finely chopped
2 green bell peppers, seeded and diced
2 green chilies, seeded and finely diced
1 garlic clove, finely chopped
1 tablespoon olive oil

Juice of 1-2 limes
8 plum tomatoes, skinned, seeded and
    diced
Salt

Mix together the diced red onions, green peppers, chilies and garlic. Add the olive oil and the juice of 1 lime. Add the tomato flesh and stir in well to slightly break down the tomato flesh. Adjust the seasoning with a good pinch of salt.

The salsa should have a good balance of flavors. More lime juice may be needed to lift the other tastes. The salsa is now ready and can be kept in the refrigerator for a few days.

Cucumber Pickle

This pickle goes very well with salads. It can be served with pork pies, corned beef or just with cold meats. But I like to serve it with fish, in particular salmon. We've all heard of smoked salmon and cucumber sandwiches, a classic combination. This pickle eats very well with simple poached salmon, but I particularly like it with Seared Peppered Salmon (p.32).

SERVES 4

4 cucumbers, peeled and seeded	1 fresh red chili, finely chopped
1½ teaspoons salt	2 tablespoons soy sauce
⅔ cup peanut oil	2 tablespoons sugar
1 teaspoon chili oil	2 tablespoons white wine vinegar
1 large garlic clove, crushed	½ bunch of green onions, thinly sliced

Grate the cucumbers on a basic cheese grater. Mix the salt with the cucumber, place in a colander and allow to drain for 20 minutes. This will take out any excess water.

Warm the peanut and chili oils with the crushed garlic and finely chopped red chili for a few minutes. Add the soy sauce, sugar and white wine vinegar and bring to the simmer. Lightly dry off the cucumber. Mix the green onions with the cucumber, then add the mixture to the simmering oil and increase the heat, stirring for 30 seconds. Remove from the heat and tip the pickle onto a deep tray or into a large cold saucepan to cool as quickly as possible. Place in an airtight jar.

Bone Marrow Dumplings

These dumplings can be eaten as a savory dish and go particularly well with pan-fried diced bacon, pearl onions and button mushrooms in a red wine sauce. They are used mostly as an accompaniment in beef stews and casseroles but I also use them with a grilled steak in red wine sauce. Just one good dumpling a portion is enough, and the beauty of using this recipe is that it keeps for three or four days if chilled. So if you want to lift just a simple, ordinary steak then have a go at this recipe.

SERVES 4

4 oz (100 g) fresh bone marrow
2 cups white breadcrumbs
2 tablespoons heavy whipping cream
3-4 egg yolks
1 heaped tablespoon chopped fresh
    parsley

A pinch of freshly grated nutmeg
Salt and freshly ground black pepper
Chicken Stock (see p.222) or water

Break the bone marrow down in a food processor, then add the breadcrumbs. Add the cream and 3 yolks with the chopped parsley. Add the remaining yolk if necessary to make a stiff mixture. Season with nutmeg, salt and pepper and chill for 1 hour before cooking to help set the mix.

Bring a pan of stock or water to the boil. The mix can be either shaped into ovals between 2 tablespoons or simply rolled into balls and dropped into simmering stock. The dumplings should be ready in 10-15 minutes. You can then add them to a stew or braised dish.

Variations

Try using other herbs instead of the parsley; thyme or sage taste particularly good.

Soda Bread

This is a recipe I tried in Ireland on my Great Food television show – another easy recipe with great results. The first time I ate soda bread, it was filled with bacon and fried egg with a big mug of tea for breakfast – it was lovely. So if you want to have a go at making your own bread for your next "full Irish / English," follow this recipe.

If you can find traditional Irish self-rising soda bread flour, all you need to add is the salt and buttermilk, but this recipe will work just as well.

SERVES 4

2⅔ cups all-purpose flour
1 tablespoon baking soda

A good pinch of salt
1¼ cups buttermilk

Pre-heat the oven to 375°F (190°C).

Sift the flour, baking soda and salt together and make a well in the center. Pour in the buttermilk and mix gently to form a dough. Knead until smooth without overworking. Lightly dust the work surface with flour and roll out the dough to a circle about ¾ inch (2 cm) thick. Cut the circle into quarters. Place on a baking sheet and bake in the pre-heated oven for 30-40 minutes until golden brown and hollow-sounding when tapped.

To cool and keep crispy, stand the bread on a wire rack. If you prefer a softer bread, wrap in a cloth to cool.

Variations

You can cook the bread on a griddle or frying pan. Heat the pan over a moderate heat. To test the temperature, sprinkle a little flour on the pan; it should turn slightly off-white. Sit the bread in the pan and cook for 12-15 minutes on each side.

Soda Bread.

Beremeal Bannocks

Another recipe from my Scottish friend, this traditionally uses beremeal, which is an ancient northern barley. If you can't get hold of it, use oatmeal or wholewheat flour. I had a go at making these while staying in Scotland. They are easy and fun to make and eat superbly.

SERVES 4-6

1 cup all-purpose flour
1 teaspoon salt
2 heaped teaspoons baking soda
1 heaped teaspoon cream of tartar

4 cups beremeal or oatmeal
4 tablespoons unsalted butter
1¼-2½ cups buttermilk

Sift the flour with the salt, baking soda and cream of tartar. Add the beremeal or oatmeal. Rub in the butter, then gradually add the buttermilk, mixing to form a soft dough. You may not need all the buttermilk; it will depend on the meal you are using.

Warm a frying pan or griddle. Shape the mix with a rolling pin or push and shape it by hand into a circle 1¼ inches (3 cm) deep; or you might find it easier to shape it into smaller loaves. Cook the bannocks directly on the griddle or in the pan over a medium heat for 2-3 minutes each side. Serve at once.

Pasta Dough

This pasta dough can be used for lasagne, fettucine, ravioli and many more pasta dishes. You can make it by hand or in a food processor. It also freezes very well.

MAKES 1 lb (450 g) to serve 4

1½ cups fine semolina or 2 cups all–
   purpose flour
A pinch of salt

½ teaspoon olive oil
2 eggs
3 egg yolks

Mix the semolina or flour with the salt and olive oil and mix well for 1 minute. Add the eggs and egg yolks and stir well until it becomes a dough. Knead the dough for 1–3 minutes until it has a smooth texture. Wrap it in plastic film and chill for 30 minutes to rest.

The pasta is now ready to use. It can be rolled, cut and cooked straightaway, or cut and left to dry and used later. If dried, the pasta will always take a little longer to cook.

More Ideas

I hope this book has given you lots of ideas and alternatives to a range of quite basic recipes. I could probably go on and on throwing ideas at you, hoping that you'll all have a go at at least one, but I have to stop somewhere. Just before I finish, though, I've got a few more for you to have a look at and think about.

Potted Salmon (see p.24) can quite easily be changed to potted shrimps. Just cook the butter with the shallots and herbs, then remove from the heat and add peeled shrimps or prawns and spoon into the molds.

Banana Ice Cream (see p.192) can be really lifted by adding 2 tablespoons of plain yogurt and 3 tablespoons of toffee (see p.164). A brilliant ice cream.

The crispy shrimp used in a skate dish (see p.76) can be used in a warm salad with lots of crunchy shrimps sprinkled over the top.

The lager-style beer batter (see p.72) can be used to deep-fry almost anything: vegetables, meat balls, sausage, fish.

Try a good Barnsley lamb chop (double chop) grilled with Hollandaise Sauce (see p.235) flavored with chopped mint and served with homemade chips (see p.22).

Calves' liver, cut into 1 inch (2.5 cm) slices, can be grilled to medium, then sliced and served with Champ (see p.134) or Dijon Mustard Mashed Potatoes (see p.91).

All the herbs I use in the book are fresh. If you can't get them, then use dried herbs tied in muslin cloth or buy the tea-bag bouquet garni.

The potatoes used in the cod dish (see p.68) can be turned into a complete starter. Just mix them with slices of red and green peppers lightly cooked in olive oil with garlic, basil, tarragon and tomatoes. Sit a warm poached egg on top of each portion and your starter is ready.

Another good duck breast dish is to score and grill the breast, keeping the skin crispy, and serve it with homemade French fries and a Maltaise sauce. This is a Hollandaise Sauce (see p.235) with a reduced blood orange juice. Straight orange juice can be used, reducing down until very strong. Add it to the hollandaise and you have an orange sauce. Serve this with the duck breast and you have a modern canard à l'orange.

Parsnips are so versatile. Once you've tried them roasted or puréed, try frying cooked parsnips in batter, like the beets on page 138.

Here's one of my favorite alternatives. If you're making one of the risottos and have some left over, spread it into a dish or tray 1 inch (2.5 cm) deep and allow it to set in the refrigerator. Once set, the risotto can be cut out with round pastry cutters (like fish cakes) or rolled into balls and dusted with flour. There are now several ways of cooking them:

shallow-fry in butter until golden brown;

roll in egg and breadcrumbs and deep-fry until golden;

dip in savory pancake mix and shallow-fry until golden on both sides.

Any of these methods will give you golden risotto cakes with creamy risotto inside. These eat well as a separate starter, with a fish or meat main course or even small ones made as canapés.

A good alternative for the Mushroom Risotto (see p.57) is to turn it into a breakfast risotto. Crispy pieces of bacon can be added or sprinkled over the black pudding sausage and then a poached or fried egg placed on top.

Here's an extra idea for the duck breast dish on page 86: just replace the parsnip with "neeps and tatties."

So that's it, I've had to stop. My whole feeling about cooking is never to be afraid of any dish or ingredient. If you believe in it, then try it.

Until the next time ...

Index

Page numbers in *italic* refer to the illustrations